The Writing on the Wall

INSIDE HIGHER EDUCATION
IN AMERICA

GAIL THAIN PARKER

SIMON AND SCHUSTER / NEW YORK

1 2 3 4 5 6 7 8 9 10

Library of Congress Cataloging in Publication Data

Parker, Gail Thain, date.
    The writing on the wall.

    1. Education, Higher—United States—History—
20th century.   I. Title.
LA227.3.P36   378.73   79-15326

ISBN 0-671-22922-2

The author gratefully acknowledges permission to reprint excerpts from the following:

"Kodachrome." © 1973 Paul Simon. Used by permission.
For Reasons of State by Noam Chomsky. © 1973. Used by permission of Pantheon Books, a division of Random House.
Presidents Confront Reality: From Edifice Complex to University Without Walls. Lyman Glenny, John R. Shea, Janet H. Ruyle, and Kathryn H. Fesci. © 1976. Used by permission of Jossey-Bass.
Academic Freedom in the Age of the College by Richard Hofstadter. © 1955. Columbia University Press. Used by permission.
The New York Times, editorial March 4, 1977. "Fewer Students Or Lower Standards." © 1977 by The New York Times Co. Used by permission.
Speedboat by Renata Adler. © 1976. Used by permission of Random House.
Letter from Dr. Alex Stewart in The New Yorker, April 13, 1978. © 1978 The New Yorker. Used by permission.

Acknowledgments

Given the nature of my conclusions, it seems only fair to begin (instead of ending) with the customary demurrer about taking full responsibility for all opinions expressed. I am deeply grateful to several dozen people who over the years have been willing to teach me and argue with me and edit my words. But I want to give particular thanks on this page to Lois Wallace and Alice Mayhew for encouraging me to publish my thoughts, and to Jessie Emmet, Alan Heimert, John McCullough, Lionel Nowak, and Rush Welter, who, in their own very different ways, have led me to believe that higher education should be something quite different from what it is today.

5

To Julia, Paul, Cassie

Contents

The curse of the public man is that he first
accommodates his tongue and eventually
his thoughts to his public position. Pres-
ently saying nothing but saying it nicely
becomes a habit. On the outside one can
at least have the pleasure of inflicting the
truth.

—JOHN KENNETH GALBRAITH,
"Maynard Keynes (rhymes with brains) and
the Mandarin Revolution," *Harvard
Magazine*

Introduction

SEVERAL YEARS AGO, when my Aunt Ruth was visiting from Arkansas, my mother took her to lunch at the University of Chicago faculty dining room. It was a particularly good day for tourists. Milton Friedman, Saul Bellow, Edward Levi, all were there, along with a hundred or so merely distinguished professors. Aunt Ruth seemed impressed—at least until the two women left the Quadrangle Club. Then she said gently, "But, honey, they're all so short."

There's a great deal to be said for looking at familiar institutions with the eyes of an outsider. And now as the columnist Nicholas Von Hoffman proclaims "Unhappiness Is a College Degree" and *The Chronicle of Higher Education* laments "New Wave of Pessimism Sweeps Some Academics: Loss of public favor, falling standards, disillusionment with accomplishment seen worrying Western scholars," it may be preferable to be a tourist in academe than a native.

But after four years as an undergraduate (Radcliffe), five as a graduate student (Harvard), three as an assistant professor (Harvard), and an unlikely four more as a college president (Bennington), I cannot hope to pass myself off as the Arkansas traveler. My perspective is that of an insider—who has the feeling that she made a rather narrow escape.

Colleges and universities can be wonderfully stimulating places, at least for the first few years. Yet there comes a time for many people when their reasons for staying on may have less to do with stimulation than with a certain failure of nerve. And those who choose to remain in academe run the danger of becoming like the patients at Thomas Mann's Sanatorium Berghof—quite willing to let someone else make all the important decisions.

The analogy with *The Magic Mountain* is unfair. Professors shop at Sears and pay mortgages just like everyone else. Certainly they display as many varieties of temperament and competence as any other occupational group. The absentminded professor is as much a stereotype as the nagging mother-in-law. Still, while few mothers-in-law seem to relish their powerlessness, professors not uncommonly express a certain pride in the fact that others—administrators, trustees, legislators—are really in charge.

Even those who think of themselves as shrewd investors or key school board members tend to act as if the business of keeping their particular college or university solvent were someone else's concern. As a group they seem not to have realized that by concentrating on their own fairly narrow interests, they virtually guarantee that institutional priorities will be set by other people who are generally more concerned with sound management than the life of the mind.

Professors complain about the bureaucratization of academic life, often with good reason. But professors have underestimated the degree to which university bureaucratization is the result of their refusal to consider the full range of interests involved in any university decision, whether the decision has to do with keeping the lawns mowed or paying the faculty.

The tremendous growth of American higher education since World War II—more students, more staff, huge new facilities—is generally cited as explanation enough for the increasing number of professional managers on campus. It does not explain why the size of most administrations continues to grow now that other forms of growth have leveled off. The need to cope with newly complex and intrusive federal regulations provides only part of the answer; hard times are often cited as an additional factor. The more troubled the seas, the more captains and first mates needed, or so the story goes.

Leaving aside the wisdom of this reasoning—too many captains may be as dangerous as too many cooks—it fails to take into account the degree to which the administrative cadre has been augmented to make up for faculty members' unwillingness to consider the practical implications of their theories about how colleges and universities should be run. As higher education has come upon hard times in the 1970s, the otherworldliness of many professors has taken on a sullen tone. A decade ago administrators were still being hired primarily to do work that was "beneath" the faculty. Today more and more managerial energy is diverted to soothe professors when possible, outmaneuver them when necessary. Academics who used to prefer to know nothing about budgets, now want to debate each line item. This would be a hopeful sign were it not for the fact that generally they still refuse to share the responsibility for final decisions. It is one thing to raise questions—quite another to be implicated.

Obviously there's a great deal of human nature

in all of this. The professors have played a more interesting game than the administrators can afford to play, perhaps than they can understand. Unfortunately both groups will be the losers in the long run, for nothing is likely to be more damaging to the credibility of higher education than the apparent inability of professors (and their administrative apologists) to prove by example that well-educated people are resourceful and resilient, disinclined to shift blame, and always ready to see that there is more than one side to an argument. Anyone who tries to follow faculty debates today is apt to come away believing that a lot of learning is just as dangerous as a little.

Consider the problem of cutting faculty size. It is almost certainly not the "right" problem insofar as it reduces a set of complex issues to mere head counting, but it is the hot topic on virtually every American campus. As uncomfortable as I am about the willingness of many administrators to imagine they're doing their jobs if the numbers add up, it makes me more unhappy to think of faculty members, who insist on fine distinctions in their own fields, trying to argue that a reduction of 2.7 percent or 7.2 percent in faculty size portends the end of Western Civilization.

I have watched the executive committee of one faculty spend three hours a week for a full semester refusing either to approve cuts suggested by the administration, or to make counterproposals, because they did not want to go on record as having acknowledged that the college was going broke. It was not that any of them believed the deficit was manageable, or that judicious reduction in the size of the faculty couldn't be made without violating contracts and damaging programs. But they knew that if they acknowledged the necessity for decisive action they would be implicated in those decisions and would be accused by their colleagues of treachery.

I sat through these meetings with the opening words of a Paul Simon song running through my head: "When I think back / On all the crap I learned in highschool / It's a wonder / I can think at all / And though my lack of education / Hasn't hurt me none / I can read the writing on the wall."[1]

Other examples of willful ignorance come to mind. Last year I heard the executive committee of a college faculty assert that (a) they were finding it hard to staff the interdisciplinary introductory courses they had just mandated because professors were already so overworked, and (b) they had been insulted by several administrators who offered to help teach the new courses—did the deans think "anyone" could teach? or perhaps they were underemployed; how else could they suggest taking on additional halftime jobs? Ap-

[1] Copyright Paul Simon, 1973.

parently it never occurred to these professors that the deans might be trying to express genuine sympathy, much less that faculty members might be the underemployed.

Walter Kaufmann, a philosopher at Princeton, has lamented the "timidity, conformity, intolerance, and the lack of high standards of honesty in academia," while speculating more generally on the tendency to blame others for what is really our own refusal to lead examined lives. Although Kaufmann does not draw an explicit connection between "decidophobia" and the virulence of faculty politics, I suspect that academics as a group are peculiarly ready to imagine that everyone is out to get them because they feel trapped by their own failure to make choices, above all the failure to leave school and go out into what they themselves think of as the real world.

"Most people," according to Kaufmann, "have failed to cultivate their critical perception of their own present position and of the alternatives they might have chosen; precisely this is the trade they made; this is what they gave up for comfort and contentment. Now they feel cheated without knowing how and when and why. What they feel is a diffuse and free-floating resentment in search of an object."[2]

For many faculty members at Bennington Col-

[2] Walter Kaufmann, *Without Guilt and Justice: From Decidophobia to Autonomy* (New York: Dell, 1975), pp. 194, 213.

lege I became that object. The president of an
institution is always a likely target, but I was particularly good at focusing their hostility. My apparent mobility—premature success, verbal agil-
ity,   access   to   airplane   tickets—reminded
members of the faculty that most of them were
stuck. The dearth of teaching jobs and, in a number of cases, their own lack of credentials, com-
bined to keep them at a college that was increasingly unsure it could afford to be interesting.

When I tried, first gently and then more directly, to suggest that their deliberations were in
fact elaborate evasions, my already troubling
presence became intolerable. The articulate,
firstborn character, who had earned the summa
and the Phi Beta Kappa key, became the witch
who had to be exorcised in the name of "community."

Knowing that the things I wanted to say in this
book would bring the academic witch-hunters
out again in full force, and not just at Bennington,
I considered trying to become the Studs Terkel
of academe. Instead of speaking my mind—and
being resented for it—I could be a good guy (at
last) with a tape recorder, transcribing the hidden
thoughts of all the decent and honest professors
who know in their hearts that something is terri-
bly wrong. I could provide them with a forum, a
very different forum from the faculty meeting
which, as longtime Harvard professor Bliss Perry

pointed out before the turn of the century, has traditionally been an intellectual wasteland.

"Is it not singular," Perry observed, "that over the question of Jones' rank, which any man in the room could settle satisfactorily enough in two minutes if left to himself, two or three dozen educated and experienced gentlemen should sit in futile misery for half an hour, only at the end of it to follow, sheeplike, some obstinate motion that takes them through precisely the wrong hole in the wall? Until the psychology of mobs gets written, there will be no understanding the ways of 'faculty action.' "[3]

By transcribing the private thoughts of professors I felt I might be able to influence notions of what it was possible for them to say in public, thereby changing, if only slightly, the shape of academic debate. At the same time I might contribute to the history of higher education by recording the feelings of academics at a time when career expectations are in flux, uncertainties about status resurgent, and professional values in the process of being redefined. I began to read Talcott Parsons.

Then I reread Terkel. His concept of the "impertinent question" seemed to be just what I was looking for. In *Talking to Myself*, Terkel describes sitting in front of his television as the

[3] Bliss Perry, "The Life of a College Professor," *Scribner's Magazine* XXII (1897): 515–16.

Vietnam War ends watching *Meet the Press, Face the Nation,* and *Issues and Answers.* A brigadier general, formerly a prisoner of war, is being questioned by two celebrated commentators. Describing "the courage of the men under torture," the general murmurs, "We all knew why we were there." Terkel assumes that sooner or later the interrogators will ask the impertinent question: "Why? Why *were* we there, General?" But they don't. The half hour draws to a close and the general "lets it be known that he and his gallant fellows are pursuing 'our national objective.' " Once again Terkel wonders if impertinence will make itself felt. "What is our national objective, General? But no, they appear to understand. I don't. I feel guilty about it, much like Algren's Some Fellow Willie."[4]

Reading *Talking to Myself,* nothing seemed more appealing than the prospect of writing a book in which I no longer spoke as the general/ college president—full of unexamined faith in national objectives and the liberal arts—but instead stepped forward as Impertinent Questioner. The one who said it all and yet could never be blamed for saying anything in particular. But having gotten this far in my thinking, I knew that I couldn't go ahead with the project. As interested as I was in finding out what individ-

[4] Studs Terkel, *Talking to Myself* (New York: Pantheon Books, 1977), p. 235.

ual professors really thought, my primary motive in even considering arming myself with a tape recorder was to find some way of saying unpopular things without being blamed. I didn't want to be Studs Terkel, I wanted to be forgiven. Terkel doesn't hide behind the people he interviews, hoping they will say things he'd never dare to.

Academics spend years learning how to barricade themselves behind footnotes. It isn't necessary to have been president of a financially troubled college to know how painful it can be to be the object of professorial scorn. Few academics manage to get their doctorates without developing a tic, a flinch of mind if not cheek, that appears whenever they make a controversial assertion they can't attribute to someone else.

Recently the story has been told of a philosophy seminar where the lecturer observed that there is no known example of a double positive's meaning a negative. A noted professor called out from the back of the room, "Yeah, yeah." It was for all purposes the end of both lecture and lecturer.[5] The implications that a narrowly competitive professionalism hold for the life of the mind (and the future of higher education) cannot be traced out in a few introductory pages. But it is clearly time to worry when a dominant voice among academic philosophers is more likely to

[5] Taylor Branch, "New Frontiers in American Philosophy," *The New York Times Magazine*, August 14, 1977.

bray a double-positive put-down, than to call out yea or nay.

The main reason I wanted to record the thoughts of other professors was to deflect the "yeah, yeahs." Worse, I had been frightened or craven enough to consider trying to argue the value of autonomy in a book designed, if unconsciously, around the superior wisdom of self-concealment. What, after all, could be more ludicrous than attempting to assert that higher education, properly conceived, should serve to augment an individual's ability to make conscious choices between alternative ideas (and implicitly, between alternative phrasings) than by publishing three hundred pages of tape-recorded free association?

Writing about conscious choices between alternatives can also be a way of hiding out, behind abstractions rather than people. Many observers of higher education sooner or later fall into what Robert Paul Wolff in *The Ideal of the University* has dubbed "the descriptive celebratory style," an "ambiguous cross between factual narrative and normative defense" which makes it impossible to be sure whether the writer is "merely recounting the changes which he perceives in American universities or is congratulating us all on them."[6]

[6] Robert Paul Wolff, *The Ideal of the University* (Boston: Beacon Press, 1969), p. 28.

My tone in the pages that follow is far from celebratory, but I've tried to distinguish between a description of things as they are and a defense of my ideas about what they should be. The first five chapters outline the ways academics protect themselves from having to think uncomfortable thoughts about the functions higher education serves or the functions it might serve. In their ahistoricism, their eagerness to believe that current practices reflect eternal verities, academics have become their own worst enemies.

The final chapter contains my thoughts about how to subvert the tendency of academics to prefer feeling wronged to feeling responsible. In arguing that both the bachelor's degree and tenure should be eliminated, I don't mean to suggest that impertinent questions lend themselves to easy answers. My conclusions may follow logically from my assumptions, I hope they do, but in the end they are dependent on a leap of faith— faith that it is always better to be aware of choices than to curse the darkness or the administration.

G.T.P.

1

The
Self-Reflexive Future

FOR ANYONE who believes that the ability to
choose between alternative interpretations and
competing goods is the mark of the educated person, there is probably no more disheartening
reading than the evasions published by academics when asked to make predictions about the future of their joint enterprise. A group of people so
conscious of the ways in which they are wronged
by insensitive administrators and an indifferent
public might be expected to welcome the thought
of a tomorrow quite different from today. Yet academic analyses of the future of higher education
are rarely millennial. In fact the professors' pre-

dictions are reminiscent of nothing so much as nineteenth-century visions of heaven. The sentimentalists imagined the hereafter in terms of picket fences and snug clapboard homes—a freshly whitewashed Norwich, Connecticut. Academics are hardly more enthusiastic about surprises.

Few in any era are sufficiently sanguine or sufficiently disgusted to think that change, any change, would be for the better. But it seems reasonable to expect that those whose business it is to grapple with unexplained phenomena and explicate unclear meanings have a more complicated way of looking at the future than a group of second-rate literary figures dedicated to the domestication of all mysteries. Professors have a professional obligation to question conventional wisdom; the sentimentalists took it upon themselves to translate such horrors as the death of a child into comforting poetic conventions, ending their stories and poems with family reunions in the sky.

Of course professors have their own methodological conventions that make it hard for them even to consider questions that don't suggest verifiable answers. Like generals they are always ready to fight the last war. And more often than not they target particular problems "significant" because they have the capacity to deal with them. During the Vietnam War, Noam Chomsky, an expert in the field of linguistics and leader in the academic anti-war movement, observed sardonically that while "Anyone can be a moral individual, concerned with human rights and problems, only a college professor, a trained expert, can solve technical problems by 'sophisticated' methods. Ergo, it is only problems of the latter sort that are important or real. Responsible, nonideological experts will give advice on tactical questions: irresponsible 'ideological types will harangue' about principle and trouble themselves over moral issues and human rights, or over the traditional problems of man and society, concerning which 'social and behavioral scientists' have nothing to offer beyond trivialities."[1]

Reminiscences about the professoriate's Vietnam War record are as out of fashion today as the rhetoric of student revolution. In Gore Vidal's words: "Current forecast: Chomsky occluded, low pressure over the black experience." It is more comfortable to forget that for every faculty dissident in the late sixties there were others eager to demonstrate that their methodologies could serve "national objectives."

A number of anthropologists and sociologists were pleased to find that they had as much to contribute to the war effort as their colleagues in applied physics. They could explain why Viet-

[1] Noam Chomsky, *American Power and the New Mandarins* (New York: Pantheon Books, 1969), p. 339.

namese peasants became less susceptible to Viet-
cong propaganda when they were forced out of
their villages and into urban slums. Generals and
politicians alike found it handy to have professors
around who knew there was no reason to nidder
about the morality of relocating entire populations. Relocation wasn't a moral question at all if
you thought of it as a research topic.

For a time it was common in liberal-left circles
to imagine that the military-industrial complex
had corrupted otherwise pure (neutral) professors. In retrospect it seems clear that whatever
seductive power lucrative consultantships or the
flattering attention of "men of affairs" may have
had, the real source of corruption was a human,
if professionally exaggerated, preference for ig-
noring ambiguities. The Vietnam War not only
gave conservative professors a chance to demonstrate their patriotism, it enabled the mavericks
among them to substitute political analysis for
self-knowledge.

Again, Chomsky probably said it best: "Those
who believe that radical social change is impera-
tive in our society are faced with a dilemma when
they consider university reform. They want the
university to be a free institution, and they want
the individuals in it to use this freedom in a civi-
lized way. They observe that the university—or
to be precise, many of its members—are 'lined
up in the service of the war technique' and that it

often functions in such a way as to entrench privilege and support repression. Given this largely correct observation, it is easy to move to some serious misconceptions. It is simply false to claim —as many now do—that the university exists only to provide manpower for the corporate system, or that the university (and the society) permit no meaningful work, or that the university merely serves to coerce and 'channel' the student. It is true that the temptation to make choices that will lead in these directions is very great. To an overwhelming extent, the features of university life that rightly are offensive to many concerned students result not from trustee control, not from defense contracts, not from administrative decisions, but from the relatively free choices of faculty and students."[2]

Chomsky published his statement of faith in 1970. It seems dated. Not, I think, in its underlying assumptions about the way the world works, but in its particular references. The "they" Chomsky refers to, concerned students and faculty members who move from "largely correct observation" to "serious misconceptions" about the difference between coercion and temptation, are hard to find these days. The same facile reasoning can be found, but the rhetoric is very different.

[2] Noam Chomsky, *For Reasons of State* (New York: Pantheon Books, 1973), p. 313.

Pauline Kael, movie critic and cultural commentator, has complained of the tendency to see
youth "as the ultimate judge—as a collective Tol-
stoyan clean old peasant." She is right, of course.
There is nothing more pathetic than the spectacle
of adults' trying to recapture youthful purity, unless it is that of youths' yearning for premature
middle age. A certain ambivalence about the
value of innocence versus experience is a source
of continual and creative tension in any college
community. The grim zeal of many of the most
talented students today, eager to do well in high
school in order to do well in college in order to
do well in law school and, presumably, in later
life, threatens this tension in a number of ways.

It reduces professors to functionaries; their
knowledge is less important than their certifying
function. In the past, some of the ablest undergraduates were drawn to academic life themselves, giving their professors a reassuring sense
of having chosen a vocation that was inherently
worthy. Now the collapse of the academic job
market means that the best students don't consider academic careers; indeed they tend to think
that their teachers weren't very bright to have
decided against medical school. Their doubts
only exacerbate the professors' self-doubts.

Perhaps more damaging still, the students are
left thinking about possible careers in the most
romantic and distant ways. Exposed primarily to

adults who have chosen an academic life (or to career counselors who have chosen to explain the outside world rather than participate in it), adolescents in college may confuse choosing a career with becoming an adult. They want to be successful doctors and lawyers and businessmen without knowing much more than what people in those categories look like.

At a trustee meeting some years ago I found myself next to a particularly incisive older woman. During a break we began to talk about the fact that of the male students who had been chosen by their fellows to come to the meeting, all but one had on a dark blue blazer and gray flannel slacks. As a group they had not yet progressed to the plaid pants stage; otherwise they had the trustee uniform exactly right.

We talked about how different it had been only a few years before when students had felt an obligation to appear before trustees dressed in savage costumes. My companion was reminded of a party she had given as an adolescent. Her grandmother, a physician and a generally formidable person, had dropped by unexpectedly. Introductions were made and the young hostess was pleased to see how gracious and mature her friends could be. Just like adults. She was sure her grandmother would be impressed—until she overheard her saying as she left: "Aren't they beautiful, and aren't they dull?"

Although I believe that the opportunity to teach should, in any reformed system of higher education, be regarded as a rare privilege, a reward for unusual intellectual or creative achievement, I am not one of those who imagine that regular contact with even the more inquiring young minds guarantees that faculty members will reexamine their own assumptions continuously. In truth, students, so far from helping to dispel the Magic Mountain quality of academic life, may actually encourage a debilitating sense of specialness in their teachers. The more highly selective the student body, the more likely faculty members are to think of themselves as the chosen who deal with the chosen.

To be sure, the student activism of the late sixties and early seventies demanded more of faculty members than the quietism of 1957 or 1977. Yet what was asked had less to do with rethinking than reacting—or acting, taking part in campus-wide psychodramas. What at Harvard was later referred to as "the time of troubles" gave decidophobic faculty members a chance to indulge in compensatory fantasies. Those who favored the war and were offended by student activists spent much of their time muttering about what they would do if a demonstrator touched them. There was more than one way to teach students a lesson. A few went so far as to dream of patrolling the libraries in the company of mastiffs.

The high manliness of the left and liberal left was often equally perfervid. Take for example an activist professor's account of a demonstration at Boston University: "So, I took the mike out of Zinn's hands and loudly and repeatedly ordered the meeting over and the ballroom cleared. . . . I was told to relinquish the mike by loud commands of 'your head will be cracked open.' I was pushed and shoved (I shoved back—in a vigorous, non-pacifist fashion) and general chaos and pandemonium seemed to take over the ballroom. My wife was seated in the audience and was in her fourth month of pregnancy. . . . I raised my voice to a very high level and, by name, charged leaders of the SDS and PL with responsibility for seeing that order be restored and that my wife be escorted safely from the ballroom."[3]

In retrospect professorial forays beyond methodology and into moral outrage were the exceptions that prove the rule. Many seem like little more than the acting out of people who ordinarily play life safe. Certainly there is little evidence that as a result of the campus upheavals during the Vietnam War academics today are any more willing to acknowledge that whatever ails higher education is in large part a result of their own free choices. A few years ago they could blame

[3] Seymour Martin Lipset and Gerald M. Schaflander, *Passion and Politics: Student Activism in America* (Boston: Little, Brown and Company, 1971), p. 343.

student agitators or the system, now they blame hard times.

There are a number of academics, of course, who preach the gospel of autonomy to their colleagues. Alfred McClung Lee, a retired professor of sociology and former chairman of the department at Brooklyn College, recently assailed his fellow sociologists for being conformists and hypocrites. In his presidential address to the American Sociological Association he suggested that the spirit of "creative dissent" is systematically destroyed by the demands of an academic career. Professors have been guilty of teaching their graduate students that only a lucky few might hope for "autonomous creativity accidentally protected by university tenure or supported by some sort of independent resources," while the rest must choose between "commitment to an orthodoxy" and "cynical acceptance of an orthodoxy as a cover for a life of hustling, or entrepreneurism."[4]

Professor Lee concluded his jeremiad with the thought that he and his colleagues must "examine and then re-examine many times and quite critically our technologies, our fanciful rhetorics, and our intellectual paradigms." I'm not sure that the rest of us can afford to wait. The higher education establishment has been able to gain time

[4] Alfred McClung Lee, "Careerism, Superficiality Laid to Sociology," *The Chronicle of Higher Education*, September 7, 1976.

by acting as if current problems can be managed away. But while they concentrate on budget cuts, reducing staff, recruiting students, general number juggling, the underlying situation grows more grave. Every year colleges and universities become increasingly opportunistic in determining their priorities, shaping curricula and degree programs according to what they think someone will pay for, and less able to afford independence of mind. Already the business of courting public favor has gone so far that words such as "excellence" and "quality" have been transformed from educational criteria to advertising slogans.

Nonetheless, if one reads reports on the future of higher education turned out by prestigious academic associations and assorted blue-ribbon committees one has little sense of trouble ahead. The technologies, rhetorics, and paradigms that Professor Lee would have us reconsider are revealed in unexamined glory. The survey is the prophetic form.

One study, conducted in the late sixties under the aegis of the American Council on Education, has been described with rare candor by the executive director of the Western Interstate Commission for Higher Education: "The technique is ingenious, but I suggest that the predictions themselves are ingenuous. They are ingenuous because they do not map out 1978 as much as

1968. . . . Traditionally, whenever higher education undertakes the task of projecting its own future, it has manifested a high degree of self-centeredness."[5]

The authors of the ACE study asked students, faculty members, administrators, and trustees to reflect on both the desirability and the probability of thirty-five options for the future. The notion that "undergraduate curricula will undergo major revisions" in the seventies was welcomed by everyone, although just what they meant to applaud remains unclear. The authors of the survey hinted at their own definition of "major revisions" in a single parenthesis: "(e.g. along multidisciplinary lines.)" A respondent who favored substantial change, but who found it hard to imagine that much could be accomplished by enlivening an introductory history course with a little cultural anthropology and regular reference to the insights of epidemiologists or statisticians would not have had any way of expressing his opinion.

Charmed as everyone apparently was by the prospect of modest curriculum reforms, there was almost equal enthusiasm in this late-sixties study for dramatic "Breakthroughs in understanding the human learning process that will lead to

[5] John Caffrey, ed., *The Future of the Academic Community: Continuity and Change* (Washington, D.C.: American Council on Education, 1969), p. 293.

major improvements in instructional methods at the college level." Not that anyone thought these breakthroughs were probable. There was no provision on the questionnaire for expressing support for changes that might fall between revisionist curriculum efforts and epistemological revolution on the scale of probability. It was as if urban planners restricted themselves to a choice between miniparks and social upheaval.

In fairness it should be remembered that *The Future of the Academic Community: Continuity and Change* was published in 1969 when, with the exception of student unrest which could be explained in terms of outside agitation and agitators, there were few signs that major changes were called for. The organization of the higher learning that had made it possible to produce thousands of new Ph.D.s every year to teach the hundreds of thousands of new students while at the same time channeling millions of dollars into new programs, college art centers, dormitories, and field houses, seemed only in need of minor readjustments.

Things have changed. Statistics gathered in 1972–74 for the federally sponsored Higher Education General Information Survey suggested that the long-term survival of 14.1 percent of the more than two thousand colleges and universities surveyed was "problematic" without "major external intervention." Another 34.8 percent were characterized as "relatively unhealthy (which might be turned around by good management)."[6]

Finances only tell part of the story. As the editors of *The Chronicle of Higher Education* have sensed, there is considerable public disenchantment with academe. Radio spots asking "Where would America be without her college-educated minds?" purport to answer their own question by suggesting that the higher education establishment has been justified once and for all by the development of an effective polio vaccine. The hidden message in this ad campaign comes across far more clearly than its official pitch. After years of boosterism, the salesmen of college education are now on the defensive.

Robert Nisbet, a professor of sociology at Columbia University, has attributed much public ill will to "an alien spirit of pride, even arrogance" among his colleagues that has compounded their failure to fulfill many of the promises they have made to society. Talcott Parsons, another sociologist, concedes "Nisbet is right that [social scientists] have failed to come up with adequate solutions for 'urban blight, poverty, racial and ethnic tensions, crime, control of the economy, family breakdown,' and other things." Yet he insists that they *have* made contributions. Moreover, as Parsons argues in his own inimitable

[6] "One in Seven Colleges Found Financially Ailing," *The Chronicle of Higher Education*, September 13, 1976.

style, "A very important aspect of the disenchantment that Nisbet speaks of can be characterized
as a deflationary reaction to a previous inflation-
ary period with its attendant recessionary characteristic of a diminution of confidence."[7]

It is easy enough to mistake demographic fluc-
tuations for cycles of enthusiasm and disenchantment. The postwar baby boom was largely responsible for the rapid growth in higher
education in the sixties. Presumably no one
would go so far as to suggest that American
women are refusing to reproduce in protest over
the failure of the educational system, but demographic figures have all sorts of subjective meanings and it is understandable that academics take
declining enrollments rather personally.

Nothing could be more depressing to a professional group than the discovery that its clientele
is shrinking. Clearly it will be increasingly difficult to justify the current size of the higher education establishment unless new students can be
found. Recognizing this hard fact, faculty members have begun to express enthusiasm for new
degree programs such as the M.A. in humanities,
programs designed to entice adults back to school
without promising them anything in particular. It
is possible to see in these new degree programs,

[7] Quoted by Malcolm G. Scully, "New Wave of Pessimism Sweeps
Some Academics," *The Chronicle of Higher Education*, November
8, 1976.

as in the burgeoning adult education movement more generally, an idealistic attempt to separate the higher learning from a narrowly conceived vocationalism. At the same time it is hard not to suspect that some of the enthusiasm is an essentially self-serving attempt on the part of academics to increase the number of potential customers.

Given "that the labor market for the educated underwent a major, unprecedented downturn in the 1970's," and that "the economic status of college graduates deteriorated relative to that of other workers, with the employment situation of the young falling exceptionally sharply," it is harder and harder to imagine that even the same proportion of a decreasing birth cohort will go on to college. Already male high-school graduates are less likely to go to college than they were a few years ago. In 1968 63 percent of them chose to become college freshmen; in 1974 only 49 percent did so.[8]

Problems of academic morale are linked to the deflation of the academic job market itself as well as to the leveling off of the professional/managerial share of the work force. Last year Kristin Helmers who runs the job office at the Modern Language Association reported that there were as

[8] Richard B. Freeman, "The Declining Economic Value of Higher Education and the American Social System" (New York: Aspen Institute for Humanistic Studies, Program on Education for a Changing Society, 1976), pp. 2, 8.

many as five hundred applicants for a single faculty position. "Even I get depressed," she admitted. "I go home at night and have a glass of Scotch and I turn on the 11 o'clock news, and then I get more depressed. I just give thanks I didn't finish my Ph.D." [9]

Presumably it was with these grim facts in mind that the Carnegie Council on Policy Studies in Higher Education undertook to publish a slim volume entitled *Presidents Confront Reality: From Edifice Complex to University Without Walls* (1976). They sent a questionnaire to approximately twenty-five hundred colleges and universities. Forty-nine percent of the presidents responded—spokesmen for institutions enrolling two-thirds of all students involved in higher education. Small colleges, religious colleges, black colleges, were underrepresented in the final sample. What was represented was the leadership of the educational establishment, and this leadership sounded almost complacent.

The history of American higher education suggests that significant institutional changes have usually been brought about by powerful individuals rather than by committees. David Riesman has recently suggested that the democratization of university governance may actually have a re-

[9] Quoted by Israel Shenker, "A Literary Gathering on a Professional Level: What Does It All Mean?" *The New York Times*, December 29, 1976.

gressive effect. In his analysis, Worcester Polytechnic Institute was able to redesign its entire
curriculum a few years ago precisely because the
various constituencies on that campus were less
inclined than most comparable groups to argue
over governance.

The students at Worcester, drawn from nearby
industrial towns and often the first in their families to go to college, were less jealous of their
"rights" than many of their peers elsewhere. The
faculty, aware of just how limited their mobility
really was, were willing to believe that their best
interests and the best interests of the institution
were closely identified. The president was a retired lieutenant general with the habit of com-
mand. Riesman concluded that conservative colleges with clear hierarchies may be more likely
to accomplish significant reforms than their more
progressive competitors.[10]

On the other hand, there is the danger that the
respect for authority that makes a college manageable may make it intellectually uninteresting.
I strongly suspect that Riesman is right, at least if
by "reforms" you mean self-corrective measures
—"humanizing" an overly technical curriculum,
combating a particular ethnocentricity, enlarging
certain programs and diminishing others. But if

[10] Anne C. Roark, "A New Curriculum Is Engineered for Techno-
logical Humanists," *The Chronicle of Higher Education*, January
10, 1977.

by "reform" you mean something more fundamental, asking questions that challenge the whole business of degrees and contracts and credit hours and focus on the problem of fostering critical intelligence, then I cannot imagine that there is any substitute for a genuinely independent faculty able to weigh proposals in terms of their effect on teaching and learning.

Historically, however, the reluctance of most professors to take responsibility for anything beyond narrowly departmental concerns made it possible for a few opinionated presidents to dominate the faculty's own curriculum debates. At Harvard, Charles William Eliot, unable to believe in the adequacy of the classical curriculum, became the great propagandist for the elective system, while at Chicago, Robert Maynard Hutchins, convinced that if truth were one there must be one best curriculum, argued unceasingly against allowing undergraduates to select their own course of study.

Oscar and Mary Handlin have suggested that "President Robert M. Hutchins' talent for pushing a good idea to absurdity exposed the limitations of general education."[11] Whatever one's own feelings about the particular issues, many of the presidents who became identified with one or more reforms possessed a similar talent. Yet it

[11] Oscar Handlin and Mary Handlin, *The American College and American Culture* (New York: McGraw-Hill, 1970), p. 79.

is they who have managed to set the terms of the discussion for generations to come, and faculty members today debate the relative worth of elective courses versus a core curriculum with as much passion as if the arguments had never been heard before.

This kind of historical perspective on the role college and university presidents have played makes it all the more painful to read the Carnegie Council report on the presidential mind in 1976. The editors of the report did not interview individuals, they sent out a survey. As a result we probably have been spared a great deal of self-celebratory rhetoric, but we are left with the two-dimensional data that can be gathered by questionnaire.

The respondents were not unaware of certain ominous signs on the horizon. "The reduction in enrollment growth has been more dramatic than many college presidents and students of higher education expected a few short years ago." "Of all institutions surveyed, about half report that their 1975 enrollments fell short of projections made in the late sixties." Full-time-equivalent student costs were up more than 10 percent annually in the period 1968–74 at a majority of the institutions responding. (Historically the figure has been 2.5 percent against dollars of constant purchasing power.) In response, extensive building programs have been shelved and faculty size has been held constant. In 1973, 65 percent of all faculty members had tenure; by 1980, the figure is expected to rise to 78 percent. Would tenure be abolished? Eight percent of the presidents said yes, by 1980. Nearly half predicted increased "rigor of standards for faculty promotions or merit increases" as well as new incentives for early retirement.[12]

But there's little need to go on with this paraphrase, for the authors of the Carnegie report were able to condense their findings into a single paragraph:

"The aggregation of responses of the individual presidents yields a basically optimistic set of views. Fewer see growth in total enrollments in the future (1974–1980) than saw them in the past (1968–1974), but fewer also see declines. Many expect to solve present enrollment difficulties by attracting adult, off-campus, and evening students. Funding problems do not dominate the views of administrators in our survey. Growth remains the expectation—not decline. Presidents hope to tap alumni, corporations, foundations, and other private sources for more funds than in the past. Although they are aware of difficulties brought on by current conditions, most presidents express confidence in the ability of their institutions to modify curricular offerings, to real-

[12] Lyman Glenny, John R. Shea, Janet H. Ruyle, and Kathryn H. Freschi, *Presidents Confront Reality: From Edifice Complex to University Without Walls* (San Francisco: Jossey-Bass, 1976), pp. 13, 14, 33, 34, 37–38.

locate resources where needed, and to otherwise plan and manage wisely, the resources available to them. No major changes are foreseen. Rather, recent changes are projected as meeting institutional and student needs of the future." [13]

Having said this, the authors of the report seem to have had an attack of conscience; at least they follow their sanguine summary with five pages of warnings. The study itself begins to read like an elaborate good news/bad news joke with the presidents telling the good news, the researchers the bad. The latter group raises not impertinent, perhaps, but sobering questions. For example, will the new adult clientele find the long-tenured survivors of a job freeze responsive to their needs and expectations? How will adult students be funded?

Then, as suddenly as they turned from optimism to candor, the authors turn back again. I can only imagine that they flinched before the anticipated "yeah, yeah" of positive-thinking academics. The study ends on a distinctly meaching note:

"Higher education provides an array of services vital to the well-being of individuals and society. It is this fact, more than any other, that leads us to conclude that despite manifold problems presented by steady-state conditions, there

[13] *Ibid.*, p. 102.

is much room for optimism. A healthier, more diverse set of institutions and post-secondary educational services will surely emerge in the years ahead. And many of the administrators who were kind enough to respond to our questionnaire will be in the forefront of that movement." [14]

There is an old saying about foundation executives—they never eat a bad lunch or hear an honest word. They rarely get a candid report either. Having filled out this particular Carnegie Council questionnaire while president of Bennington, I know that the only way you could show that you understood the seriousness of the situation was to admit that your own institution was in peculiarly lousy shape, a nearly impossible admission to make.

College and university presidents, like all people who bear the burden of explaining away difficulties and heartening the troops, gradually become incapable of turning off their public voices. When I think of the energy I poured into explaining why Bennington College was worth six or seven thousand dollars a year, how it wasn't elitist to have a high tuition (after all, one *could* be taking from the rich to support the poor through scholarships, one just didn't happen to be able to afford to do so), and then when I think of those presidents who have everything invested in a

[14] *Ibid.*, p. 108.

role they have spent years understudying for, it is no wonder that they seem to be reading from well-thumbed scripts when asked to speak their minds.

Professors have more latitude; they can be openly pessimistic and even spiteful. But the intense personalism of faculty debate does not, in fact, allow the participants to speak more directly than their former colleagues who have become administrators and talk in descriptive-celebratory phrases. Probably the most provocative historian of higher education today, Laurence R. Veysey, has suggested that "what academic men did *not* say" at any given time probably was as significant as what they did say. An agreed-upon verbal etiquette was the sign that the higher learning in America had come of age, having developed a clear enough form of its own to serve, in Veysey's words, as "an agency for social control."

"The custodianship of popular values comprised the primary responsibility of the American university. It was to teach its students to think constructively rather than in an imprudent and disintegrative independence. It was to make its degrees into syndicated emblems of social and economic arrival. It was to promise, with repetitious care, that the investigations of its learned men were dedicated to the practical furtherance of the common welfare. It was to organize its own affairs in such a businesslike fashion as to reassure any stray industrialist or legislator who chanced onto its campus." [15]

My only quarrel with Veysey's analysis is that it seems inconceivable to me that the university as it currently exists is in any very direct sense the creation of stray industrialists who happened to be trustees or stray legislators who approved budgets. Our colleges and universities were created primarily by the choices of the academics themselves.

Kenneth Dolbeau, writing on faculty power in *Academic Supermarkets: A Critical Case Study of a Multiversity*, has suggested that "For the most part, faculty have not seen education in any terms except those the society sets for it—vocationalism, adaptation to the ongoing society and economy and their needs, and the means to mobility and status." But he is forgiving. The system is too much for an institution, much less an individual, to buck. "It is hard to see," he writes, "how a university which receives its support from state and federal governments, follows the established values and practices of the society, teaches the orthodox beliefs of the established disciplines, and prepares students for places in an ongoing social and economic order can be anything but a completely nonneutral agent of the present status quo. The only thing remarkable

[15] Laurence R. Veysey, *The Emergence of the American University* (Chicago: University of Chicago Press, 1965), pp. 440–41.

about such status is that many people apparently
define total integration in the surrounding society
as neutrality."[16]

One sign that the war record of the academic
community is not quite forgotten, just repressed,
is the way in which neutrality has been aban-
doned as a professorial rallying cry. The old ideal
of the disinterested scholar was brought into
question during the late sixties as it became increasingly clear that individual professors, like
the academic institutions they worked for, were
so thoroughly implicated in the war effort that
most claims to neutrality seemed somewhat silly,
even sinister.

As a result there has been a complete about-
face, and the ideal of disinterested scholarship
has been replaced, at least for publicity purposes,
by the image of the professor who can inculcate
values in the hearts and minds of the young. In
fact this has been less an about-face than a 360-
degree turn, for the notion that the professoriate
can serve a quasi-priestly function was central to
nineteenth-century theories about the ways in
which a college education built character.

In the next chapter I try to explain the repeti-
tiveness of higher education in terms of an ahistoricism on the part of most academics. Preferring

[16] Kenneth M. Dolbeau, "Faculty Power," in *Academic Supermarkets,* Philip G. Altbach, Robert S. Lauter, Sheila McVey, eds. (San
Francisco: Jossey-Bass, 1971), p. 166.

to think of their educational theories as existing
out of time or any specific context, many professors repeat not only history but themselves. In
the following pages, I consider how the new-old
emphasis on teaching values (formerly thought of
in terms of character building) shapes current
curriculum debate. But here my concern is less
with past and present than with the self-protec-
tive way academics have analyzed the future,
whether as researchers or as respondents to a re-
searcher's questionnaire. In this connection the
debate over neutrality provides one more illustration of how people skilled at dealing in abstractions can use this skill to avoid explaining their
choices to outsiders—or to themselves.

Kenneth Dolbeau suggests that the myth of academic neutrality has given the great majority of
professors an opportunity to imagine that they,
unlike their fellow citizens, could rise above
their own mixed motives to a kind of magisterial
disinterestedness. In some cases, of course, individuals have been able to do so. Yet often, professors as a group have mistaken an occasional
triumph of pure reason for a permanent habit of
mind, and have not been as careful as they might
about scrutinizing their own complicity with the
status quo.

Predictably, the myth of neutrality has been
embraced by faculty dissidents as well as those
who would prefer to imagine that they came to

their majoritarian opinions by Olympian logic. Robert Paul Wolff, trenchant critic of the descriptive-celebratory style and mocker of those liberals who justify their preference for piecemeal reform as "pragmatic" or "hard-nosed," writes in his book *The Ideal of the University* that when it comes to academic reform "the honest and consistent course is not always the best." As a prescription for institutional behavior, value neutrality suffers "from the worst disability which can afflict a norm: what it prescribes is not wrong; it is impossible."[17] Yet Wolff feels it would be a mistake for radicals to bring this mythical norm into question because they benefit more from it than any other segment of the university community.

It probably isn't necessary to review the whole ambiguous history of the professors' involvement in the Vietnam War or to read every complacent report on the future of higher education or to try to disentangle the various arguments that suggest that academic neutrality is the refuge of professorial Babbitts *and* the last best hope of dissidents in order to come to the conclusion that many academics are given to ingenious self-justification.

In his autobiography Benjamin Franklin told of how he gave up vegetarianism while on a voyage.

[17] Robert Paul Wolff, *The Ideal of the University* (Boston: Beacon Press, 1969), p. 70.

The odor of frying fish was finally so tempting that he found himself thinking that if big fish eat little fish then he was perfectly justified in eating the big ones. How "convenient a thing it is to be a *reasonable Creature*," he concluded, "since it enables one to find or make a Reason for everything one has a mind to do."[18]

Still, for all Franklin's slyness, he never tried to argue that one had a right to ignore the probable consequences of one's decisions. And it is this carelessness of consequences, rather than self-centeredness *per se*, that seems to me most disturbing about academic habits of mind. Few human beings are capable of saintly disinterestedness, but a willingness to try to predict the possible effects of one's choices (or nonchoices) seems the least that can be expected from those who are paid to educate. In a certain sense the stereotype of the absentminded professor may be more kind than cruel.

[18] Chester E. Jorgenson and Frank Luther Mott, eds., *Benjamin Franklin: Representative Selections* (New York: Hill and Wang, 1962), p. 34.

BUSINESS RECORDS

BANKRUPTCY PROCEEDINGS
SOUTHERN DISTRICT

Thursday, Dec. 16, 1976
Petition filed by:

MARCIA ELAINE KLUGMAN, 652 W. 163d St., N.Y. Liabilities, $9,710.00; Assets, none.

RICHARD R. MOYSEY, Box 4, New Paltz Road, Highland, N.Y. Liabilities, $8,802; assets, none.

PATRICIA A. MOYSEY, Box 4, R.D. 2, New Paltz Rd., Highland, N.Y. Liabilities, $8,802; assets, none.

CARLOS CASTELLANOS, 2406 University Ave., the Bronx, Liabilities, $1,900 to be repaid (Chapter XIII.)

FINCH COLLEGE, 52 E. 78 St., N.Y. Liabilities and assets not listed. Rodney Felder is president of the corporation.

HECTOR RODRIQUEZ, 2342 Ryer Ave., the Bronx. Liabilities, $2,378; assets, none.

AMY C. TUMALE OEHLKERS, 40 E. 86 St., N.Y. Liabilities, $7,723; assets, $662.

PAULA ANN THORPE, 1470 Jessup Ave., the Bronx. Liabilities, $16,461; assets, $775.

WILLIAM C. BEADLE, 3 Monroe Place, Port Chester, N.Y. Liabilities, $5,909; assets, $901.

ELLEN BEADLE, 3 Monroe Place, Port Chester, N.Y. Liabilities, $5,909; assets, $901.

CLOIE M. GREEN, 4 E. 107 St., N.Y. Liabilities, $13,528; assets, $722.

*Chapter XI petition for an arrangement
by:*

ELECTRO FINISHING INC.,   13
Haven St., Elmsford, N.Y. Liabilities,
$795,201; assets, $495,800. Signed by
Ronald Schor, president. Business is
refinishing and painting of office
equipment furniture and accesso-
ries.[19]

---

[19] *The New York Times*, December 16, 1976.

2

The
Self-Reflective Past

WHILE ANALYZING hysterical patients, Freud
discovered their symptoms might be "overdetermined," that is, they could be traced to two or
more sufficient causes. The inability of academics to conceive of a future for higher education
that differs significantly from the present is similarly overdetermined. Not that it is a hysterical
symptom. It may make sense to speak of "the academic mind" when referring to a common body
of published lore or a characteristic kind of reasoning, but efforts to identify group neuroses are
dubious.

All I mean in applying the concept of overdetermination to academic habits of mind is that there is more than one explanation for the professors' reluctance to pose impertinent questions or come up with uncomfortable answers. If I were trying to analyze why some people become professors and others don't, it would make sense to speculate about what unconscious needs academic conservatism might serve. But because my intention is to suggest how most professors think about certain problems (and what problems they are likely to ignore), little purpose would be served by sketching a group psychological profile.

In preferring sure things to risky things, academics are no more craven than anyone else, although their instinctive preference for the familiar is strengthened by their favored methodologies. In short, they are both human and human beings who have learned not to raise certain kinds of questions, at least in public. But there is still another explanation for the reluctance of most faculty members to envision significant changes in academic policy or practice. More than one hundred and twenty-five years ago, Henry Tappan, an early president of the University of Michigan, observed that American colleges tended to look alike.

> We set about putting up the same kind of buildings, we create the same number of professors to

teach the same things on the same principles; we get together a few books and some philosophical apparatus; and then we have the same annual commencements, with orations and poems, and the conferring of degrees; and we get under the same pressure of debt and make the same appeals to the public to get us out of it.[1]

The need for instant traditions was only too real in Tappan's day. New colleges were springing up all across the country, testimony to local or denominational pride, and unless they looked right, had all the usual facilities and rituals, they couldn't hope to attract students. Lacking traditions of their own, they simply borrowed them from Williams or Bowdoin, hoping some of the older schools' élan would rub off in the process.

Unfortunately, over the years what was necessity has come to be seen as virtue. The instant and imitative traditionalism of the academic community has itself become a tradition, reflected not only in campus architecture but in the habits of mind of the academics themselves. And it is their ahistoricism, their refusal to see that the particular forms characterizing American higher education today grew out of specific historical contexts, that makes it so hard for them to imagine that changes in the economy, for example, may re-

[1] Quoted by John Caffney, ed., *The Future of the Academic Community* (Washington, D.C.: American Council on Education, 1969), p. 10.

quire commensurate changes in academic life. Looking to the past only to reinforce their sense that current academic practices have a suprahistorical inevitability, they have few clues about what factors to consider in making realistic predictions about the future.

Robert Paul Wolff, who defends the myth of neutrality from the radical point of view, has managed both to mock and to exemplify the essentially narcissistic way in which academics use history. In *The Ideal of the University* he makes fun of his colleagues for their willingness to invoke great thoughts in order to avoid minor personal inconveniences. His favorite example of "this extraordinary narrowness of vision" comes "of course" from the University of Chicago where Robert Hutchins managed to ensure that some portion of the "Great Conversation," his term for the interchange of seminal ideas down through the ages, would be paraphrased in the course of every faculty debate. "Some while ago, the question was raised in a meeting of the Chicago College Faculty whether history should be added to the contents of the general education program. A dedicated acolyte of the Tradition rose to argue against the proposal. In support of his position, with medieval deference to authority, he quoted from *Poetics* in which Aristotle argues that history is an inferior discipline because it deals only in particulars, whereas poetry deals in universals." The view lost but, to Wolff's amusement, it was regarded as entirely relevant.

Wolff himself is honest enough, however, to admit to a taste for that cultivated man or woman "on whom allusion is not lost, in whose discourse there echo earlier voices, one capable of that special sort of irony which comes from the awareness that one's most precious thoughts have been anticipated."[2] Hutchins could not have put it better.

Wolff's willingness to be self-critical, to use the word "taste" to describe his convictions rather than insisting on their eternal rightness, seems admirable, as far as it goes. I wish he'd gone on to suggest how great a difference there is between feeling humbled by earlier voices and feeling smug for being able to make out what they are saying. It is that humility we refer to when we say someone is "philosophical," while it is that smugness that reduces so much academic discourse about quality to quibbling over style.

Faculty members, deans, and college presidents are so apt to mistake good form for taking a position, to confusing matters of etiquette with those of intellectual integrity, that it would be easier to convert the editors of *Women's Wear Daily* to the truths of affirmative action than most

[2] Robert Paul Wolff, *The Ideal of the University* (Boston: Beacon Press, 1969), pp. 7–8.

academics. Those journalists who have assured us that Jacqueline de Ribes' nose, old Sonia Rykiel cardigans, and Pierre Berge's dog, Moujik, all have style, almost certainly know more about their own prejudices than the professor who calmly announces, "I never notice whether a candidate is a man or a woman," as if this were evidence of anything other than self-involvement.

Professor Wolff gives the game away when he talks about his own taste for cultivated men and women. He reveals, if inadvertently, how academics transform the history of ideas into a species of personal adornment, a talisman against the unfamiliar. One's most precious thoughts have been anticipated. Everything has been said before. Enthusiasm is in bad taste. Noam Chomsky has suggested that academics find moral fervor unacceptable because they have a professional commitment to concentrate on those problems that can be solved by sophisticated methods. Wolff offers a second explanation: enthusiasts lack a saving sense of irony.[3]

Traditionally there has been one exception to the distaste for zealotry; it has long been re-

[3] In certain respects these two explanations reflect the thinking of scientists (Chomsky) as opposed to humanists (Wolff), yet throughout I have chosen to blur two-culture distinctions, believing that while people in different fields are likely to choose different strategies of avoidance, in the end the results are largely indistinguishable, and equally destructive of the ability of the academy to analyze either its function or its failings.

garded as proper form for academics to suggest
that their professional perquisites are among the
bulwarks of democracy. Just as individual faculty
members dress up convenient arguments with
snippets from the Great Conversation, the profession as a whole has tended to welcome interpretations of the history of American higher education that prove the central importance of its joint
enterprise.

Until quite recently, that history has consisted
for the most part of handsomely bound commemorative volumes heralding decades (or even centuries) of achievement. And the few histories
written for a professional audience echoed the
theme of ever onward and upward. Perhaps the
best example of academic history as self-fulfilled
prophecy is Richard Hofstadter's *Development of
Academic Freedom in the United States,* long regarded as a seminal work and only recently criticized as "Whig history of the most blatant kind,
written from the future where historical changes
seem simply 'inevitable' and the past teems with
'revolutionary turning points,' 'watersheds,' and
'cures,' all heralding the 'dawning of new eras'
and death's 'transfiguration.' "[4]

Even more disturbing than Hofstadter's Whig-
gery is the way in which he allows his interpretations of historical events to be skewed by his

[4] James Axtell, "The Death of the Liberal Arts College," *History of
Education Quarterly,* Winter 1971, p. 341.

eagerness to show that whatever is admirable in academic life or rhetoric today is firmly rooted in tradition. In the first volume he observes that the concepts currently associated with academic freedom were at best nascent before the rise of the university, as opposed to the liberal arts college, toward the end of the nineteenth century. "The modern idea of academic freedom has been profoundly affected by the professional character of the scholar, by the research function and scientific conceptions of the search for truth, and by the manifold services, aside from teaching students, that are rendered to the community by the great university."[5] Despite this reminder that past and present are not a seamless web, Hofstadter makes such adroit use of the "if only" technique that the reader is tempted to imagine that if only the American Association of University Professors had been on the scene, the Civil War itself could have been averted.

Hofstadter is careful to avoid any direct assertion of causality, relying instead on "symptom," "token," and "illustration" to imply connections. "By the 1850's," he writes, "the South had lost its ability to take realistic stock of social issues. While the absence of freedom in its halls of learning was only one of the symptoms of this loss, it was a token of a severe general intellectual paral-

[5] Richard Hofstadter, *Academic Freedom in the Age of the College* (New York: Columbia University Press, 1955), pp. 261–62.

ysis. The cost to the South, to the nation at large, from the incapacity of Southern leadership to take a more liberal and rational view of the immense problems arising out of slavery and the sectional conflict, was tremendous. The history of the antebellum South is a cogent illustration of the principle that the maintenance of intellectual freedom is not of concern to the intellectual classes alone, but is of central importance to all members of the community."[6]

Who could disagree, at least if the champions of academic freedom are assumed to be willing to argue for the extension of their privileges to everyone? But problems emerge when Hofstadter moves from statements of first principles to give specific examples. In 1856 Professor Benjamin Sherwood Hedrick at the University of North Carolina had the temerity to argue the cause of the Republican party. His brave words were just that—he had no opportunity to vote for the Freeman ticket in North Carolina. Nonetheless he was burned in effigy by students, hectored by the press, and finally dismissed by the trustees.

On the face of it, Hedrick's story seems to support Hofstadter's thesis about academic freedom —if only. . . . But Hofstadter is too honest a historian not to admit that "there were very few native Southerners in academic posts in 1856 who

[6] *Ibid.*, p. 259.

would have cared to challenge the South's peculiar institution or the mores connected with it.
They would have sworn that to be unable with
impunity to espouse 'lunatic' notions like Hedrick's was no real deprivation of liberty. They
had, in short, subjective freedom on this issue.
But there is no condition more dangerous to a
community than subjective freedom of this kind
without objective freedom."[7] What exactly does
this mean? How does one encourage "objective"
freedom?

There is an enormous difference between what
Hofstadter knows to be true—that few professors,
no matter how well-protected, are ever likely to
mount a sustained assault on the status quo—and
the impulsion of his rhetoric which seems to
suggest quite the opposite. That difference is
clearer when he considers the case of antebellum
professors living above the Mason-Dixon line.
"While a number of Northern colleges were in a
sense 'abolitionist' colleges and thus contributed
much to the moral agitation over slavery, the academic culture of the Northern states did not
make a striking contribution to a rational discussion and sober exchange of views on the possible
solutions of the slavery question. In part this was
a product of their traditional curricular practices
and their neglect of advanced sociological in-

[7] *Ibid.*, pp. 258–59.

quiry. But in greater part it must be attributed to the absence of sufficient freedom and detachment."[8]

If only there had been a scientific sociology, if only there had been sufficient freedom, if only professors could rise above the prejudices of their fellow men. Even a historian as skillful as Richard Hofstadter has difficulty writing a history of higher education that is not crudely self-projective: the mythologically free university professor, striding through the ages, making all the difference, if only he'd actually been there.

Less real harm probably has been done by handsomely bound commemorative volumes or complacent academic histories than by the tendency to imagine that a handful of colleges and universities embody both the past and the future of the entire system of higher education. The number of people reading, much less the number writing, academic histories is relatively small. But there are many who believe that tradition is in residence at a few of the most prestigious institutions and who therefore measure the validity of all reform against "the way they do it" at Princeton or Stanford or Wesleyan. Insofar as this ahistorical perspective has confused standards with standardization, it has had an even more inhibiting effect on attempts to reappraise the prospects

[8] *Ibid.*, p. 261.

of individual colleges and universities than the self-congratulatory volumes published to commemorate "centuries of excellence."

By depicting the history of higher education as a process of revelation in which certain timeless principles were gradually unveiled, Hofstadter may have reinforced academic narcissism. Yet Whiggish historians have simply projected back over time their contemporaries' eagerness to believe that current academic practices have a historical inevitability.

The uniformity of these practices may seem dismal to the outsider, but to the insider, it is welcome proof that they must be right. Henry Tappan observed a certain instant traditionalism in academe more than a century ago. Style and substance are still confused. If our new gymnasium has the same kind of flexible seating as Brown University's field house and we have the same faculty contract system as the University of Wisconsin, we must be doing something right. Or is it that we only have a protective coloration?

Because the rituals of the more prestigious institutions are passed down through the whole system as the standard, I have felt little hesitation about drawing most of my bad examples from these schools. My reasons for quoting almost exclusively from faculty members at "major universities" and "leading colleges" are similar—with one additional twist. It is easy enough to get

copies of curriculum reports, student news-
papers, capital fund brochures, and admissions
office materials from any school. But it is virtually
impossible to read what the majority of faculty
members are thinking, whether about their own
specialties or the true nature of the higher learning, because they don't write.

According to their own report, two-thirds of the
half million faculty members in the United States
have never published a book or monograph.
Finding out what is on their minds is very different from finding out what a Chomsky or Wolff is
thinking. You have to go talk to them—and do the
editing yourself. This is not only time consuming
but raises in my mind all sorts of uneasy questions about violating privacy, taking advantage of
hospitality, and generally not doing unto others.
It has always been hard for me to understand how
anyone could be an anthropologist, entering into
dialogues, entering into other people's lives, with
a determined double consciousness. No doubt
my horror of the whole business has been exaggerated by a few experiences with journalists
who seemed to want to understand my point of
view only to quote me out of context in some
melodrama of their own concoction.

Suffice it to say that I've written the next few
pages with distinctly mixed feelings. In them I've
tried to show the forms academic ahistoricism can
take in the minds of faculty members at a relatively obscure college. The obvious way of find-

ing out what these professors are thinking would have been to mail them a questionnaire. That way I wouldn't have to meet them face to face. But it seemed dishonest to me to illustrate the academics' tendency to think about their customary practices as if they existed without reference to any particular historical moments, with anonymous information gathered without reference to any specific educational contexts. Instead I have tried to put in all the details, perhaps too many to protect my subjects from identification. All names, needless to say, have been changed.

The drive from the Fort Wayne Airport was flat and straight. Only one elbow in the road, in front of a perfectly square farmhouse. There's a woman in there, or so I was told, who decorates her house and lawn for every holiday. Christmas brings Mary and Joseph, angels, Santas with reindeer, lights; Easter means plastic eggs dangling from every tree and an outsized bunny with a basket. It was almost Easter, but the yard was bare. The woman behind the wheel, wife of Berghof College's president, seemed concerned. "Maybe she's away on vacation this year," she said to her friend Selma in the back seat. "I sure hope she's not sick. I've always wanted to go meet that woman and thank her for putting up the only show worth looking at on this road." Selma nodded.

Every Thursday the two women drove to Fort

Wayne to eat breakfast, have their hair done, do a little shopping, have tacos at a favorite lunch stop, and then head back home. It was, as they put it, their "outing." The rest of the week the president's wife performed her duties. Most recently she had invited the three rival ministers of Berghof's denomination to dinner the Sunday before Easter. "Pray for me, Selma," she said. Selma laughed.

That night I ate dinner with the president's wife, the president, and assorted faculty members before going to a "faculty development meeting." Someone at the table slyly mentioned that the presidential couple had been seen at a Johnny Cash concert in Kokomo the night before. The president smiled weakly and put his head in his hands. His wife explained that she had not only dragged him to the concert, but had written a note to Johnny Cash beforehand saying how much she liked the way he shared his faith. Cash had dedicated his second song to her.

The president, wincing and grinning, began to pound his forehead with the heel of his hand. There was no real laughter around the table, just a ripple of practiced amusement. The presidential couple apparently had a well-rehearsed routine: she embarrassed him, he mocked himself for being manipulated by this large blond woman. It was a bit of theater with deeper meanings. From what I'd heard about the paternalistic way in which Berghof College was run, it was no doubt cathartic for the faculty to see their leader put in his place.

There were limits to the fun, however. It was one thing to see the president wince, it was another for the professors to have to wince themselves. The president's wife clearly believed anyone was fair game. Clever as well as Christian, she began to tell them how interesting it had been at the Johnny Cash concert to see real working people up close and feel their enthusiasm. One faculty member raised his eyebrows and asked if there were "working people" these days, implying that at sixty-three he alone could remember what it meant to work. Another began to talk about Cash's music. Several got onto the subject of rock and roll.

There was a theater performance scheduled after the evening's faculty meeting—a repertory group from Cambridge presenting a musical version of *Gulliver's Travels*. Reportedly the music was rock. No one could like that kind of music, they said; it was too loud. The man who had tried to analyze Cash's appeal switched quickly to "the horizontal as opposed to the vertical structure of rock." That's why you don't like it, "it's not because it's so loud, it's that you can't hear it going anywhere so you don't know when it's going to be over."

"You're all such snobs," the president's wife

said. They nodded happily. "Yes," replied one, "we really are cut off from the real world." A chorus of pleased assent. "We're really much closer to the Cambridge people than to the people around us." The chocolate and pineapple pudding pie was finished. It was time for my performance. As the faculty gathered in a basement room, I tried to express my uneasiness about the tendency of academics to think that if an idea sounded right then it *was* right, while anything that violated their educated expectations was wrong. Those who questioned tenure were as outrageous as rock musicians.

As luck would have it, the president had on the Countess Mara tie of office, while a wiry, white-haired biology teacher had on a red bow tie. I suggested that beneath these seeming idiosyncrasies was a profound standardization, that every college had a Mara-crested president and a bow-tied biology professor. There was some uneasy laughter. Mostly from the young dissidents who had their sandals on in mid-March.

It was time to be more direct. They had flown me to Fort Wayne in order, I quote, to "broaden their horizons." I had read their curriculum revisions, proposals worked over for two years, and I suggested that it troubled me somewhat that they were indistinguishable from ones made elsewhere. Harvard, Amherst, this Midwestern stronghold of an obscure denomination, they all looked alike, at least on paper. Wasn't it possible that different institutions should be different by design, not just by default? Didn't it seem odd that colleges serving very different students should share such a uniform sense of what should be taught and how best to teach it?

Feeling my missionary powers at a low ebb after the pudding and pie crust, I tried quoting David Riesman on Worcester Polytechnic. How did they think the faculty at Worcester felt when they read that their inability to find other jobs, in combination with their respect for authority in the form of an ex-general become president, was what had made reform possible? Was Riesman's analysis of the ways in which a basically conservative college might find it easier to change than a more innovative one relevant to Berghof? No one seemed to have anything to say. I passed out small sheets of paper and asked everyone to answer a few questions.

1. What is your field? How old are you? How long have you taught at Berghof?
2. How would you characterize the college's financial health? Are there problems recruiting students?
3. What proportion of the faculty could find comparable academic jobs elsewhere within a year and a half? Could you?
4. Do you feel that significant changes will have to be made in the curriculum within

the next ten years, changes of a different order of magnitude from adding a non-Western Civilization requirement, or offering three interdisciplinary introductory courses? (These were their new curriculum proposals.)

5. If you answered "yes" to #4, how do you think the shape of the future will be determined: by trustees, administrators, faculty members? In other words, who will make the decisions and by what process?

6. If you had three wishes for Berghof College what would they be?

Not a probing research instrument, but a set of questions that I hoped would help broaden the faculty members' sense of what it was permissible to say—and think.

I read their answers out loud to them, seeing if I could discover patterns as I went along. Unfortunately, those patterns were only too clear about five minutes into the discussion. According to the faculty, there was no economic reason why anything should change at Berghof. The budget had been balanced for seventeen years. One person referred to the administration as "tightfisted," two-thirds of them used the terms "good," "stable," "very good," to describe the financial situation, the other third characterized it as "OK," "fair," and only one felt things were going to deteriorate rapidly. One faculty member wrote,

"better than might be expected." As I was reading the answers out loud I remarked, "The Real-
ist." Later I was sorry. The first of his three
wishes was for seventy endowed faculty chairs.

Opinion was split somewhat differently on the
question of student recruitment. About half felt
there was some problem, whether with the quality or the number of applicants. Slightly more
than one-quarter felt there was no problem; if
anything, things were looking up; slightly less
than one-quarter were distinctly pessimistic. I
asked whether they knew what the admissions
figures actually looked like. They didn't. Yet they
had little sense that a vague uneasiness about admissions might color their outlook on finances.

Responses to the question on faculty mobility
—could your colleagues get comparable jobs
elsewhere? could you?—reflected much the
same tendency to avoid uncomfortable thoughts.
More than 65 percent of the faculty believed that
their colleagues had a better than even chance of
locating new jobs expeditiously. Two-fifths were
willing to bet on a 75 percent chance or better.
The youngest and oldest faculty members were a
little less sanguine than the rest. Presumably
those under thirty-five had had some firsthand experience of the current job market, while those
over fifty-five knew that they were too old to
change jobs, and no one wanted to rate his colleagues higher than himself. Those in the mid-

dle-age ranges preferred not to think of themselves as trapped, no matter how comfortable the incarceration. Nor did they want to feel like murderers when they didn't promote a junior colleague. Their psychological needs could only be satisfied by the dream of mobility.

Intriguingly, 60 percent of the faculty members at Berghof rated their own chances for finding jobs even higher than those of their colleagues. Approximately 10 percent sidestepped the question by saying that there was no way they could imagine improving their lot, they were "above mobility," while another 15 percent rated their chances as zero. With one exception, a forty-one-year-old philosopher who had only been at Berghof a year and who therefore had a certain grim realism about the job market, all of the zeros were within ten years of retirement.

There *was* evidence that some faculty members knew more than they were telling. The social scientists believed that they personally had an 85 percent chance of finding alternative academic employment in a year and a half, the scientists gave themselves just better than 70 percent (on the average they'd been at Berghof twenty years), and the members of the professional disciplines were willing to bet on odds of slightly less than 2:1 in their own favor, but the humanists believed they had only a 27.5 percent chance of getting out.

In part this can be accounted for by age spread: the average age of faculty members in both the humanities and the social sciences was forty-two, but while the median age of the social scientists was also forty-two, that of the humanists was fifty-one. Moreover, in a small college the experiences of the newly hired philosopher were no doubt well known to colleagues in allied departments. Still most faculty members had repressed whatever information they did have about the job market. Certainly they did not seem able to generalize with any accuracy about their colleagues or to capitalize on the desperation David Riesman celebrated—if we're all going to be here for the next twenty years, we had better ensure that we are doing something different to attract students and renew our self-esteem.

On the subject of major change within a decade, the humanists divided evenly, the scientists tended to say no and refer to school traditions (of course they themselves were among the traditions), the social scientists were evenly split, and the professionals were more inclined than most to believe it necessary to "keep abreast of the times." Yet a number of the teachers of professional subjects were the most conservative proponents of strong liberal arts requirements. Over the years they no doubt had discovered that the rhetoric of liberal arts defense was their own best justification for staying in an academic environment, rather than actually producing radio programs, running small businesses, or teaching handicapped children.

Some faculty members responded to the question—where will change come from?—even if they didn't expect any change. Here too the votes divided evenly. One-third felt that the president or the administration would have to come up with the ideas as well as the plans for implementation, one-third felt that either the faculty as a whole or a few individual faculty members leading the rest would be the motive force behind major changes, and the final third suggested some hermaphroditic device—a joint committee, a mutual process of exploration, a dialogue.

Given these responses, it is hardly surprising that the faculty and administration at Berghof College could only tinker with their curriculum after two years of deliberation. In addition to their pride at being identified with the "Cambridge people" and their zeal to make their curriculum resemble the latest turn of the screw at Harvard, they relished the thought of being true to their own time-honored ways. There is no paradox in this; they could never separate their academic traditions from those of the "leaders" because these traditions were expressed in out-of-time, out-of-context, standards-standardized terms. Quality, excellence, depth, and breadth, these *were* their traditions. And just to make sure that these abstractions never took on any radical meaning, indeed any meaning in particular, over the years they had developed a kind of ritual dance that they did whenever the curriculum chant began. The faculty would divide into three groups, enough pessimists to partner the optimists, while the great majority sat right down in the middle of the floor.

This well-rehearsed performance with no surprises made me eager to get on with the three wishes. Here, if anywhere, was a chance for someone to improvise. It was a chance not taken. Despite the widespread lack of financial concern, more faculty members wished for money than anything else. In some sense, I suppose, this was like using one of your three wishes to wish for anything that might occur to you later. It was the wise child's answer to the fairy-tale proposal. But what is shrewd behavior in a six-year-old may be unbecoming in an adult. To wish for money was, in this case, to avoid choosing anything in particular.

Those few faculty members who tried to suggest what they wanted the cash for revealed more about their own best interests than any notion of the greater good. Some wanted science equipment, others studio space, library books, a gym. Only 10 percent of the faculty wished for higher salaries—they were already upper middle class in rural Indiana. No one mentioned a need for more scholarships or for keeping tuition rates down. In the light of their concern about admissions this seemed odd, if unfortunately characteristic.

After money, the second most popular wish was for a change in college governance. There was considerable interest in having more faculty participation in decision-making, more democratic procedures, a greater reliance on majority vote and less on assumed consensus. Some bluntly suggested "a new dean," others a more innovative and visionary administration in general. In the discussion on this point no one seemed to have any idea that there were trade-offs involved. They were primarily concerned about the face-saving possibilities of participatory democracy and unwilling to consider the possible advantages (that long-balanced budget?) of a hierarchical structure. All they knew was that while their curriculum was indistinguishable from that at prestigious schools and therefore "correct," their committee structure was embarrassingly out of style.

Third in popularity after money and democracy was a wish for more students—with a few votes, very few, for better ones. This was not a faculty eager to improve the quality of the student body. Many of them had gone to Berghof themselves. They were comfortable. The denominational affiliation of the college ensured that a number of students enrolled every year who could have gone to more selective schools. A few faculty members suggested the need for more student discipline or wryly mentioned the increase in boozing among the student body. Only one faculty member longed for a more diverse group of students—livelier, more sophisticated.

He was the same one who wanted a more diverse group of colleagues, although two other youngish professors hinted darkly at the need for "new blood." There was some interest, but very slight, in raising standards for tenure. One brave soul wanted to do away with tenure altogether. Or perhaps he wasn't so brave. I suspect from what he said about his field and age that he was the faculty member who had just been denied promotion. A lone scientist wanted greater emphasis on research. All in all, there was little enthusiasm for upgrading the faculty despite some interest in expanding the sabbatical system to include paid leaves for learning new things.

There were just about as many people interested in curriculum reform as in upgrading the faculty, but here the responses were even more fragmented. Some wanted to loosen graduation requirements, others mentioned the need for independent study, interdisciplinary courses, courses "looking toward the future," reducing the number of courses and majors. A handful went beyond talking (implicitly) about a more student-centered curriculum to mention the need for a stronger student voice in governance, but their inclinations were counterbalanced by another handful who advocated more rules and regulations, emphasis on basic skills, exposure to "real-world occupations," all in the vocabulary of the medicinal dose.

Finally there was an expression of interest in sharpening the college's sense of mission, making it clear just what its religious commitments were. But again everything came out even. For each faculty member who wanted a less parochial student body and faculty, there was one who wanted a more homogeneous group with a shared sense of sectarian purpose. For each one who wanted to loosen up the curriculum in the name of student choice, there was someone else who felt that the basics had been ignored; for the advocate of student power there was a temperance vigilante.

Standing there in front of the Berghof faculty with all the little piles of paper in front of me, I began to see that this parlor game I had initiated in the name of faculty development had been played out along lines as well-rehearsed as the dinner conversation. The president, the heavy father, made a fool of by his wife. The advocate of science safely held in check by the advocate of art, the optimists by the pessimists, the dissidents by the contented, each side counting on the other to keep the play going and to hold everything in place. No one had missed a cue. It was time to see *Gulliver's Travels.*

Neither did I miss my cue the next morning when the president's wife and Selma were driving me back to Fort Wayne. At dinner one of the deans had whispered, "Be sure to ask the president's wife to tell you the story of the blue punch." It sounded like something out of Poe. I couldn't resist. Apparently she used to travel all over Indiana giving a monologue that involved putting on thirty different hats. Once when invited to address a local sorority she had noticed that the hostess's front door was swagged with white and blue. Inside she saw that the table had a blue and white floral arrangement. So did the mantel. Later, when she went into the bathroom and saw that the toilet water was dyed blue, she began to realize what the sorority's colors were. But the real giveaway was the punch. It was exactly the same blue as the toilet water. And that, you guessed it, was the punch line.

By this time we had slipped around the elbow in the road to Fort Wayne and into the parking lot of a restaurant. I had time to eat breakfast with the two women before they dropped me at the airport. In the middle of our poached eggs the president's wife asked, "Why is it that professors always have something to say about the difference between horizontal and vertical music when you're trying to talk about Johnny Cash? Why do they always bring up all that information, more information than anyone wants to know? Women professors aren't so much that way," she added tactfully. "They seem broader somehow; they can talk just like anyone." Selma began to nod vehemently. Apparently her father-in-law and her brother-in-law were both Berghof professors. She had had a bellyful.

"Well," I said hesitantly, "sometimes people who feel ill at ease seek refuge in books." I was so conscious of trying not to lecture and wanting to be a credit to my sex, that I could barely speak. "Maybe all the information is a kind of defense, an attempt to hide behind superior knowledge."

Suddenly the president's wife and Selma began to talk about what kind of little boys the professors they knew must have been. They eagerly seized the idea that they were fundamentally ill at ease. Thinking of these self-important men as shy seven-year-olds must have given them the same satisfaction my Aunt Ruth felt when she realized that the professors at the University of Chicago were short.

Then I realized why the dean had insisted that I ask about the blue punch. He was sure that the story would damn the president's wife in my eyes, proving that her perspective was that of a woman with thirty hats. She provided the comic relief and reminded them all of their intellectual superiority. But in fact what she reminded me of was that those academics I'd eaten with and talked to the night before seemed incapable of any perspective at all. Theirs was the politics of complacency, taking sides to ensure that nothing happened. Ask a question, any question, and there'd be twenty for, twenty against, and forty right in the middle.

If Robert Paul Wolff gave the professorial show away when he described the charm of knowing it's all been said before, a place like Berghof gives the whole higher learning away. My own prejudices in favor of autonomy, even impertinence, make me want to believe that those faculty members who express doubts about the status quo are the more incisive thinkers. But it is the majority at Berghof who are actually closer to the truth.

The professors who wanted their college to differentiate itself, to become more denominational, more secular, more anything, had my sympathies. Yet those who would rather have Berghof look right than look different were in some sense more realistic. Their realism may have been inadvertent, in fact it probably was. Nonetheless, in welcoming standardization they were making it possible for their college to survive, at least for the time being.

The same ahistoricism that makes so many academics welcome instant and imitative traditions makes it possible for them to adapt their institutions to serve a job-screening function in American society. And it is that function more than any other that has stimulated public support for mass higher education. Academics have developed their own reasons for following standard practices, reasons that grow out of status concerns rather than any analysis of just what role colleges and universities play *vis-à-vis* the job market. They have never had to say to themselves, "O.K., if we're being paid to discriminate without seeming to be discriminatory, we'd better do everything we can to convince the public that our standards are standardized."

In truth, if academics had ever said this to themselves, they couldn't have done a better job of getting their act together. The difficulty is not that colleges and universities, at least the great majority of them, have not been admirably adapted to hand out essentially interchangeable credentials, but that this adaptation has taken place without forcing the professors and presidents to understand just what the relationship is between higher education and the job market. As a result, as that market changes they will be almost totally unprepared to deal with the repercussions.

Fred Hirsch in *Social Limits to Growth* has made a number of observations about the economy that seem crucial to me in seeing the dangers of believing that higher education can serve as an effective job-screening mechanism. Hirsch begins his analysis by distinguishing between the material economy "defined as output amenable to continued increase in productivity per unit of labor input," and the positional economy which "relates to all aspects of goods, services, work positions, and other social relationships that are either (1) scarce in some absolute or socially imposed sense or (2) subject to congestion or crowding through more extensive use." [9]

As far as Hirsch can see, only the material economy is still growing. Having a giant Winnebago is a material good—you pay your money and you have the camper of your dreams. But a summer home with a private beach is a positional good; there are limited numbers of them. And building more cottages on a given stretch of shore simply decreases the desirability of them all.

As a family's income rises, goods and services that are primarily positional in value attract a higher proportion of their total budget. "Prominent examples," according to Hirsch, "are expenditures on education, vacation housing, and a variety of personal services." [10] Obviously the word "positional" has a number of connotations, but whatever Hirsch himself may think about the in-

[9] Fred Hirsch, *Social Limits to Growth* (Cambridge, Mass.: Harvard University Press, 1976), p. 27.
[10] *Ibid.*, p. 28.

herent worth of owning an isolated summer home, he makes it clear he has his doubts about the value of education when it is conceived in primarily positional terms. In fact he laments the way in which higher education has come to be thought of as a "defensive necessity," something you want not because having it will give you pleasure, but because it will help to keep other people from getting ahead of you.

As Hirsch points out, there is enormous social waste involved in defensive education; resources of time and money are absorbed in an ever-lengthening screening process and, in the end, individual expectations are generally disappointed. From the point of view of the higher education establishment there are compensations —in the long run students may be disappointed, but in the short run they (and their parents and the government) pay their tuitions. Certainly the wisdom of those who would try to make every Berghof a Beloit and every Beloit a Williams is apparent. A positional good is a positional good is a positional good—at least in comparison with a merely material good.

Ironically, the expansion of the higher education system after World War II, and particularly during the 1960s, has ensured that a smaller proportion of college graduates can look forward to summer homes and superior jobs, for the growth in the number of graduates far outstripped the rate of growth in the positional portion of the economy. Hirsch suggests that the only way to counteract the current tendency to overinvest in educational credentials is to recognize the difference between material and positional goods and to distinguish between material rewards and positional jobs. In other words, jobs that are regarded as inherently rewarding should not also be the best paid.

He suggests introducing a Dutch auction system for allocating positions in the professions and upper echelons of business, bidding down salary levels to the point at which available openings are just filled by a suitable number of qualified applicants. The satisfactions of being a doctor or lawyer or professor should be regarded, in Hirsch's scheme, as a form of compensation in themselves. There is no reason why these fortunate professionals should be bribed with above-average salaries in addition.

In fact, if you follow his analysis, there is every reason why professionals shouldn't be bribed. If credentialism has already damaged higher education, it will almost certainly do more harm as the positional economy shrinks and the "worth" of degrees—as that worth is commonly defined —grows more dubious. Using college degrees as vocational tests has involved losses both to education and to what Hirsch refers to as "its unprofiting victims. It is another facet of the modern affliction of doing even luxury things not for their own sake but as a means to something else."[11]

The presumption is that once the best jobs were no longer the best paid, candidates for degrees would be those "who enjoyed the education itself." And higher education would be far less vulnerable to devaluation based either on fluctuation or long-term cycles in the economy. It would be heartening to think that professors would join Hirsch in deploring the waste of resources and expectations involved in continuing to accept the fact, even tacitly, that college, degrees are primarily valuable as evidence that the bearer survived a job-screening process. In fact, there are signs that academics are beginning to deal with the overwhelming evidence that degrees no longer guarantee access to the good things in life. Talk of the cash value of education is out, values are in, and the case for higher education is more often argued in terms of the need to teach ethical precepts to the young than in terms of the obligation to provide for their upward mobility.

But the new rhetoric seems more a rationalization than a real change of heart. Certainly the redefinition of "value" is a step in the right direction, but it would be a more significant step if it reflected an attempt to come to grips with the way higher education actually functions in society, in-

[11] *Ibid.*, p. 184.

stead of just a sophisticated play upon words. As things stand there is something about the crusade to restore the value of the degree by teaching values that is reminiscent of all the futile efforts to put the Christ back in Christmas.

The City University has begun a crash drive to corral warm bodies into its classrooms. Enrollment has been declining precipitously, and since some state aid is pegged to the number of students, university administrators are worried. If applications don't pick up, they may be compelled to make cutbacks, which could adversely affect many careers. So they have decided to make admission easier by assorted forms of salesmanship, and a lowering of the high school average required for admission to one of the senior colleges, from 87-80.

Much as we sympathize with the university's predicament, we cannot help but remember the warnings from educators some years ago that affirmative action programs would inexorably drag down levels of scholarship. The introduction of ill-prepared students into a college, they cautioned, must mean either unkind failure for the students or unhealthy compromise for the college. Those cautions had force at the time and the present body hunt gives them force today. We are loath to think that the educators who deplored the lowering of standards then will remain quiet now merely because their own welfare is at stake.[12]

[12] *The New York Times*, March 4, 1977.

3

The
Self-Projective Curriculum

OVER THE YEARS the standardization of American academic life has served two primary functions: it has made it possible for academics to imagine that a relatively comfortable status quo reflects eternal verities and for nonacademics to believe that higher education is a reliable and essentially fair way of screening candidates for jobs. Henry Tappan described one kind of uniformity, the uniformity of appearance. As long as all the usual buildings were built, professorships named, and commencement rituals followed, few inside or outside the academy would question either the worth of a particular institution or of the degrees it awarded its graduates. Today it is even easier to see in the standardization of higher education a marketing strategy, a means of assuring outsiders that the insiders *must* know what they're doing.

But there is another kind of uniformity that functions primarily to allay the uneasiness of insiders, assuring faculty members that they and they alone are making all the crucial educational decisions. It is the interminable and essentially circular debate over curriculum reform. If administrators wanted to ensure that the intellectual and political energies of the professoriate would never be brought to bear on genuinely interesting or troubling questions, they could do no better than to set them arguing over the proper ratio of required to elective courses, the just balance of departmental interests, and the legitimacy of new fields of study.

In fact there has been no sinister cabal on the part of administrators. The professors themselves, unwilling to become involved in the discussion of those questions that require making choices that cannot be unmade a year or five years later, have preferred to spend their time wrangling over the curriculum. An uncharacteristically acerbic foundation report described the situation in some detail:

> One of the great indoor sports of American faculties is fiddling with the curriculum. The fac-

ulty can engage in interminable arguments during years of committee meetings about depth versus breadth. They can fight almost without end about whether education should be providing useful or liberal knowledge. They can write learned books and articles about the difficulties of integrating human knowledge at the time of a knowledge explosion. And of course the battle between general and specialized education is likely to go on until the end of time. Curricula are constantly being changed. New courses are introduced, new programs are offered, new departments are created (to quickly become powerful vested interests of their own), sequences of courses are rearranged, honors programs are introduced, catalogues are rewritten, teaching loads are adjusted, and a grand and glorious time is had by all.

The harsh truth is that all this activity is generally a waste of time as far as providing better education for students is concerned.[1]

Anyone who has taught at the college level for more than a semester could turn an outline like this one into a forty-page script. Take the question of faculty advising for example. When course sequences are altered or new programs introduced, the opponents of change invariably protest that faculty advisers are already overtaxed.

[1] Hazen Foundation report, *The Student in Higher Education*, 1968, quoted by James D. Koerner, *The Parsons College Bubble* (New York: Basic Books, 1970), p. 35.

How, they ask, can we require our colleagues to assume new burdens of explanation? In response, the supporters of the proposed curriculum reforms have a choice of answers—either A or B.

A. Our proposals will neither make the situation better or worse. If the advising system is near collapse we'll have to look into it. Later.

B. You're right. One of the beauties of our proposal is precisely that it makes the inadequacy of the current advising system so clear. Vote for our reforms and then we'll work out a new counseling scheme.

A retired faculty member at Bennington has observed that there will be counseling at the college as long as the faculty needs it. Counseling or advising fills a variety of needs. It gives those conscientious professors who are not active in their fields a way of feeling overworked. They may only teach eight or ten hours a week and prepare for those classes another ten hours, but they have filled up the rest of their days advising. Drinking coffee with a student becomes an act of self-sacrifice when it is thought of as counseling. Moreover, by arguing the need to be ever available to students, nonpublishers can get back at their more productive colleagues. If advising is a sacred obligation, then every scholarly article is an act of treachery, a violation of one's responsibility to the young, an attack on the spirit of community.

Advising can give professors a sense of being good all-round human beings, something difficult to be sure about when you spend your time writing snide book reviews or grading papers. It is an opportunity to empathize; unhappily it can be hard to distinguish between empathy and exploitation. The sexual possibilities are among the less alarming. Sitting alone with students, questioning them about their course selection and life plans, it is easy to blur the distinction between evaluating academic progress and evaluating character. And when students come looking for advice about their work they often find their personality being assessed—and subtly threatened.

I remember one girl at Bennington who was annoyed by an adviser who urged her to make regular appointments and then maundered on and on, asking her how she really *felt* about her family and her roommate and her lover and her other professors. One day in exasperation she said to me, "I never know what ——— is really trying to get at." Having just had lunch with ——— it so happened that I did. "I think he wants you to hand in your two overdue papers." "Well, Jesus," she exploded, "why doesn't he just say so?"

There is no question but that an attentive and sympathetic faculty adviser can make a great deal of difference to a student. The problem lies in distinguishing between what is useful to the student and what a professor, projecting his or her own needs into the counseling situation, might like to imagine is useful. Given the essentially narcissistic habits of mind that many faculty members bring to analyzing the past and future of higher education, it is hardly surprising that the debate over the curriculum (and the subdebate over advising) can be understood best in terms of faculty as opposed to student needs. Year after year, while ostensibly arguing over what to teach, faculty members go about the business of defining and redefining their relationship to each other and to the outside world. Unfortunately in this case, the medium—curriculum debate—is pretty much the entire message.

Recently there has been a well-publicized resurgence of interest in requirements and so-called core curricula. After a dazzling rise in the sixties, Charles W. Eliot's elective stock is down; the smart money is on some version of Hutchins's Great Conversation. Why the change of heart? Simple reaction? Having pushed the elective idea to absurdity in the late sixties, a certain retreat was inevitable. Yet there is a deeper dynamic at work, one that grows out of a pervasive sense on the part of academics that their stock in general is deflated. They seem to think that if they can define what core of information an educated person should know they can restore public faith in the idea that higher education itself is the very core of American culture.

Fritz K. Ringer, writing in *The Decline of the German Mandarins,* has described the way in which German academics in the first thirty or so years of this century tried to counter steady public devaluation of their enterprise. The parallels between their chosen lines of defense and the rhetorical strategies of American academics today are instructive. Ringer's Mandarins contended that only professors could be relied upon to interpret those sacred texts that were the source of true German culture. "They regard [ed] learning as a process in which contact with venerated sources result [ed] in the absorption of their spiritual content, so that an indelible quality of spiritual elevation was conferred upon the student," and, no doubt, upon the priestly intermediary as well.

The German Mandarins spared no ingenuity in trying to prove that professors had a crucially important role to play in preserving values in an era of moral chaos. Richard Hofstadter's tendency to write as if academic freedom were the basis of all our other freedoms seems an innocent enthusiasm in comparison with the efforts of the German academic community between the world wars to prove that they had a monopoly on the eternal (Germanic) verities. "In examining the German academic pamphlet literature of the Weimar period," Ringer writes, "one is struck, above all, by a frantic sense of engagement. . . . After 1921, the professors tried harder than ever to show that they were not mere specialists and that their work had elevating implications. Thus an astronomer felt compelled to move in a page and a half from spiral nebulae to the historical right of existence of the German Empire."[2]

It would be melodramatic to suggest that talk of "values education" leads inevitably to resurgent national chauvinism. Yet in arguing for a return to core courses, grand syntheses of ethics and history, morality and nature, and in resurrecting the "whole man" ideal (ostensibly on behalf of overspecialized, vocationally oriented students), American faculty members today are trying above all to reassure themselves that they are invaluable members of society.

To read over the paeans to the whole man uttered by educators during the last one hundred years is an excellent way of seeing how the Great Conversation, in the mouths of the self-justifying, can become the Same Conversation—noble thoughts reduced to cant. In 1870 the president of Amherst, William Stearns, summarized the collegiate ideal for his contemporaries: "We propose

[2] Fritz K. Ringer, *The Decline of the German Mandarins: The German Academic Community, 1890–1933* (Cambridge, Mass.: Harvard University Press, 1969), pp. 9, 384–85.

a liberal in distinction from a specific education; a symmetrical, and, as far as the possibilities of a four years' course will allow, a complete education. We are not schools of knowledges and informations so much as of training and culture." [3]

Fifteen years later, Daniel Coit Gilman, the president of Johns Hopkins, expressed the hope that the American university would never become "merely a place for the advancement of knowledge or for the acquisition of learning; it will always be a place for the development of character. A society made up of specialists, of men who have cultivated to the extreme a single power, without simultaneously developing the various faculties of the mind, would be a miserable society of impractical pessimists, it would resemble a community made up of boys who can paint portraits with their toes, who can calculate like lightning, who can remember all the hats of all the guests in a fashionable hotel or perform innumerable feats on the tight-rope."[4]

As president of Johns Hopkins, the first American university to insist on the importance of original research and academic professionalism, Gilman played a significant part in the trans-

[3] Quoted by George E. Peterson, *The New England College in the Age of the University* (Amherst, Mass.: Amherst College Press, 1964), p. 27.
[4] Daniel Coit Gilman, "The Relationship of the University to the Progress of Civilization," *Report*, University of New York, 1886, p. 210.

formation of American higher education from an assortment of ill-equipped colleges to an essentially hierarchical system with a handful of major universities at the top. He hoped that this new order wouldn't mean the death of the whole man. But by the turn of the century it was clear that the universities had a more successful product to offer than the well-rounded college boy— the trained specialist. Recently, however, as increasing numbers of Ph.D.s are discovering that specialization may be a liability in a tight job market, graduate school brochures are beginning to read more and more like paraphrases of Gilman. Elective courses on ethical and social issues are being added to the curricula of professional schools and cross-registration between these schools and graduate programs in arts and sciences is being encouraged.

On the face of it, this attempt to produce something other than narrow specialists seems a clear step in the right direction. Few of us are without the suspicion that our world is currently being run by boys who can paint with their toes. Yet it is possible to see in all the talk about ethics courses for professionals and in the development of new master's programs in the humanities just another attempt on the part of historians and philosophers and professors of literature to attract warm bodies to their classrooms. Unquestionably some of the enthusiasm for resurrected core courses, whether for undergraduates or would-be lawyers, has been the result of sagging enrollments, particularly in the humanities, the supposed home of values.

Members of the American Historical Association have been quite open about their motives, at least within their own councils. At the 1976 AHA convention, historian William H. McNeill warned colleagues, "Our discipline is in a perilous state, in danger of losing the privileged position it has enjoyed in highschool and college curricula." When Stanford University dropped its Western Civilization requirement approximately eight years ago, the number of students taking upper-division courses in history and the number of history majors were cut in half. In the light of this and similarly depressing data from campuses across the country, Professor McNeill encouraged his fellow historians to develop an introductory course that could be replicated at every college or university, for "If we cannot agree on an introductory course then we are simply saying to the rest of academia that we have nothing worth teaching." Too many historians, he suggested, have been offering students a "rich diet" of their private researches. "The only thing that can save us is to find something worth teaching to undergraduates *en masse*—something the educated person should know. . . ."[5] Something, one might

[5] Quoted by Karen J. Winkler, "An Era of Decline for History?" *The Chronicle of Higher Education*, January 10, 1977.

feel, analogous to the strategies adopted by Volvo for selling cars.

In the academic bull market of the 1960s, professors discovered that it was far more convenient to teach one's specialty than to have to learn a little about a lot of different things in order to introduce freshmen to the life of the mind. And as students expressed more and more interest in designing their own programs of study without being bound by requirements, the proliferation of highly specialized courses on the undergraduate level could be made to seem a sign of respect for student maturity, rather than a matter of professorial convenience. Why insist that every freshman take Introduction to Western Civilization? Freshmen were so much more sophisticated than they had been even a few years before. Let them pick and choose as they will—we trust them.

Of course in the sixties the professors had two stays against anarchy—and unemployment. There were the residual rules left over from the General Education enthusiasm of the fifties. Foreign language requirements were rapidly disappearing, but in general there was enough of the old structure left to ensure healthy enrollments in fields such as history. More importantly, there were plenty of students to go around. Worries about filling courses or majors and thereby justifying one's existence on the payroll were virtually unheard of. Now that the demographic

picture has changed, so has the faculty reasoning.

This about-face has been made official by an
article in *Time* magazine (April 1977), our "National Poet Laureate" as Robert Coover (*The
Public Burning*) puts it. Beginning with the
"Manifesto of Liberal Arts College Presidents,"
"We believe that the conditions of our time force
us to recognize the distance between what we
say liberal arts can do and what it is now doing,"
the article goes on to herald the resurrection of
required courses. Everybody's doing it. Harvard,
Cornell, Georgetown. The president of Middle-
bury College put the case for a core curriculum
most bluntly: "Parents and alumni love it, because it reaffirms the idea that the institution
knows where its values lie. And yes, what their
money is being spent for." Exactly. What could
be more welcome, at a time when the cash value
of a college education seems to be dropping precipitously, than the proposition that the value of
the whole enterprise can be reaffirmed by teaching values?

I would never want to argue that close study of
great ideas and books is anything other than
worthwhile. Yet I have difficulty with the common professorial assumption that because they
themselves have spent years studying they hold
the keys to both vocational and spiritual king-
doms. Individual members of the professoriate

may serve as mentors in the fullest sense, but as Max Weber warned against the pretensions of German Mandarins, it is dangerous for students to regard professors as "all-round coaches in the business of living."[6]

If regular contact with the noblest thoughts of man were guaranteed to have an elevating effect, the professors' own councils would be characterized by disinterested probity. With the exception of a handful of academic historians, however, few have suggested it would be a great leap forward if public debate were modeled along lines established in faculty meetings or American Historical Association conventions.

The opposite case was put most strongly by Catharine Esther Beecher more than a century ago. She dreamed of establishing a separate and distinctly female institution of higher learning, in large part because of her disgust with comtemporary academic politics. In *Truth Stranger Than Fiction: A Narrative of Recent Transactions, Involving Inquiries in Regard to the Principles of Honor, Truth, and Justice, Which Obtain in a Distinguished American University* (1850), Beecher told the story of a woman wronged by the professoriate.

Her heroine, frequently compared by students to Madame de Staël's Corinne, became the friend

[6] Quoted by Ringer, *op. cit.*, p. 354.

of a young man at the Yale Divinity School. Nothing more than friendship seemed possible; he was ten years her junior. But as Catharine Beecher tells the tale, he insisted on an engagement. The woman resisted, until finally they had been seen together so often that she felt she had to give some account of her behavior. Only under intense social pressure did she reveal the engagement to a few close friends. When her explanations got back to the young man, however, he vehemently denied any formal agreement and declared himself the victim of her practiced arts.

"From the first day of its publication," Beecher asserts, "this tale of monstrous scandal, unsupported by a shadow of proof, contradicted by all the evidence in the case, was sent forth on its cruel errand, under the sanction and protection of at least five University Professors and their families."[7] The plot thickened. When the young man was put on trial before his ministerial association (at the insistence of the maligned woman's brother), the jury was packed with professorial partisans. Just before the crucial vote, one of these partisans went so far as to hint to a wavering colleague that the lady had once said *he* had been her suitor. The young man was acquitted.

[7] Catharine Esther Beecher, *Truth Stranger Than Fiction: A Narrative of Recent Transactions, Involving Inquiries in Regard to the Principles of Honor, Truth, and Justice, Which Obtain in a Distinguished American University* (Boston: Phillips, Sampson & Company, 1850), p. 155.

Scandalmongering is endemic in small towns
—and university enclaves are no exception. What
is peculiar to the academic community is the malice that is freely expressed in public discourse.
Small-town gossips operate behind closed doors.
Professors mimeograph manifestos and speak
openly to colleagues and student reporters alike.
"Professor ———'s charge in last Tuesday's faculty meeting that the Committee of Six is guilty
of 'asinine pedantry, moral insensitivity, and continuous meddling' has fostered confusion among
faculty members." "Assailing what he called the
administration's 'absurdist philosophy,' mathe-
matics department chairman ——— charged high
University officials" with transforming "a fac-
ulty-run University to a Multiversity dominated
by a special administrative caste without real responsibility to the faculty."

Occasionally faculty members are apologetic
about what must seem to any outsider a striking
lack of self-perspective. When the director of the
Center for Black Studies at the University of De-
troit was interviewed by *The Chronicle of Higher
Education* (November 29, 1976), she contrasted
her priorities in the 1960s with her priorities ten
years later. She had been "a militant black
leader" demanding what she and fellow black
students felt was just and right. "It was a lot easier to be an outsider in the '60s because you could
holler and scream. I did it very well, and I enjoyed every minute of it." But more recently she

had spent considerable time worrying about the cost of faculty parking. "It's been a big concern of mine this year," she confessed, "and I can't believe this is me."

Her story is a classic illustration of what happens when an outsider becomes an academic insider and loses a certain sense of proportion in the process. What confirmed insiders have to say about the significance of their particular institution often suggests that they suffer from delusions of grandeur. For example, when an alumnus of one major university questioned whether the institution's commitment to blacks justified her sending a contribution, the university's vice-president replied: "If this place had to lower its standards, the entire civilization of the world would suffer. . . . You asked about why you should support the place. To me the answer is quite simple: it is the best. I wish I shared the privilege you have, of having been the student of this place. If you choose not to give any more, that is your business. But I am arrogant enough to think the business of life is everyone's and I think you ought to thank God for what you have had here."

Although this particular administrator's prose goes beyond the merely celebratory, it would be a mistake to imagine that faculty members are not deeply implicated in official onanism. Because they can speak with open malice about any and all administrators does not mean they are self-critical. Their complaints about the growth of an administrative caste whose members make decisions without first consulting the faculty are full of crocodile tears. The truth is that the professors as a group have been unwilling to bear the burden of understanding what the relationships are between salary increases, tenure policies, tuition, financial aid, sabbaticals, core courses, teaching load, and so forth, and have defaulted on what are properly their decision-making responsibilities. As a result the day-by-day determination of how resources should be allocated increasingly has come to be made by those whose training and predilections lead them to analyze problems from the point of view of sound business practice.

I do not suggest that concern for the bottom line *in itself* unfits a person for educational administration. On the contrary. But there are different ways of making sure that the bottom line isn't written in red ink, and the ways that seem most logical to M.B.A.s and lawyers may not make much sense to those whose primary commitment is to scholarship and teaching. Administrators who argue against deficit spending are not necessarily philistines, wretches, the sworn enemies of scholarly values. Yet unless faculty members are able to enter into these administrators' proper concerns about institutional solvency *and* take responsibility for discovering alternative

ways of attaining that goal—ways they feel preserve the integrity of the intellectual operation
better than constant haggling about professorial
productivity, faculty/student ratios, contact hours,
and the like—they have themselves primarily to
blame for the emergence of a separate and powerful caste.

In addition, professors must share a certain
amount of blame for the manner in which administrators have gone about the business of ensuring that the resources are there to divvy up. By
a combination of intransigence and selective ignorance, faculty members are responsible for the
claims made on their behalf, whether they are
the slick words of the admissions counselors, the
half-truths of the fundraisers, or the relentlessly
optimistic statements of presidents determined to
find something to make parents and alumni and
legislators happy.

When faculty members claim to *be* the college
or university, they are quite right. But like the
Berghof faculty's demands for participatory democracy, their claims are hollow unless they are
clearly understood to include obligations. The
professors at Berghof College showed few signs
of being willing to accept the responsibilities of
participatory democracy, the obligation to understand, for example, how the admissions picture
affects the financial health of their school and ultimately touches on their own interest in subsidized "faculty development."

This selective understanding characterizes much faculty thinking at the more prestigious institutions as well. The appointment of an academic to the presidency of Yale inspired one of his colleagues to remark that the average professor has administrative experience equivalent to that of the head of a medium-sized corporation. His point was that one didn't have to be a dean, much less a lawyer, to know how to run things. Yet the fact remains that no matter how many committee meetings professors may chair in their lifetimes or how many curriculum proposals they may draft, their responsibilities are quite different from those of someone who is the chief executive officer of a business, no matter what its size. Professors specialize in making decisions that can, indeed almost certainly will, be remade, by the next special committee or faculty senate. People who manufacture ladies' wear or sell real estate don't have this luxury.

A particularly striking example of willful ignorance among faculty members emerged in an exchange over salaries reported recently in the student newspaper of a leading college. Last spring the president of the college circulated a memo which he unfortunately referred to as "self-explanatory." The trustees, he reported, had changed the wording of one of their earlier resolutions in response to faculty pressure for "clarification." The original statement read, in part: "The Trustees' general objective is to maintain faculty compensation at a level not lower than other institutions of highest quality so that ─── will remain capable of attracting, retaining, and suitably compensating eminently qualified faculty members."

Because some professors had read the resolution to mean that the college would maintain salaries competitive with Ivy League schools, while others believed it measured compensation against preeminent undergraduate institutions, at the president's suggestion the resolution was amended to read: "The Trustees' general objective is to maintain faculty compensation at the level of comparable institutions of highest quality"; in short, Williams not Yale. "The wording of the old statement was never ambiguous," protested the acting dean of the faculty in a faculty meeting. "It made no distinction between a college or a university as a competitor." "I would have rather lived with [the dean's] illusion than your reality," added a second faculty commentator, looking pointedly in the president's direction.

Inflation in the seventies, coming after a period when professors' salaries were increasing rapidly in relation to previous compensation and cost of living, has made the debate over further increases particularly acrimonious. But the whole issue of salaries is heated because of the way higher education has functioned in the American

economy—not just because of the way that economy fluctuates. Historically, no matter how loath
professors have been to think of themselves as
mere credentialers, they have not gone out of
their way to undermine the notion that college
degrees guarantee success in later life.

In part this is just one more illustration of their
tendency to mistake historical accidents for eternal truths. Yet it also reflects the fact that certain
assumptions about the cash value of degrees have
proved too useful to the professoriate to make
them want to ask hard questions. Faith that degrees guarantee upward mobility, at least until
very recently, has ensured public support for
higher education. And it has also provided faculty
members with a particularly convenient way of
arguing for salary increases; after all, shouldn't
those who certify others for success enjoy subtan-
tial rewards themselves?

In 1893 William Rainey Harper published an
article on "The Pay of American College Professors" in which he struck to the heart of the matter.
After the usual (at least by now usual) laments
that the salaries of professors compare unfavora-
bly to the wages of "skilled workmen employed
in the mechanical industries," Harper observed
that "The business of college professors requires
not only talent, training and equipment, and dili-
gent application to the work in hand; it requires
also the maintenance of a social standing. In this

respect," he suggested, "it differs from most other occupations. . . . The mechanic may be equally serviceable in any rank. In the professors' craft, under modern American conditions, this is not the case. His work, the aggregate of his influence on those whose instructor and, to some extent, exemplar he is to be, will suffer if his social standing suffers."[8]

In other words, it is only proper that those who screen young people for vocational success should themselves be visibly successful. Otherwise they will suffer the fate of elementary-school teachers, treated as servants by their wealthier students. At a number of colleges today, where the average student spends on tuition, room, board, and stereo equipment more than half of what the average professor earns, there is an unpleasant tendency for the students to insist on the tribute owing those who are "paying for it." On these campuses there is so much grumbling about the accommodations that it is easy to imagine oneself on a Russian ship surrounded by German tourists.

Of course Harper's shrewd assessment of the importance of ensuring an upper-middle-class life-style for professors is valid only as long as higher education is primarily seen as a process for determining who is worthy of white-collar employment. If the link between future income

[8] W. R. Harper, "The Pay of American College Professors," *Forum*, September 1893, p. 108.

and degrees is broken, whether on purpose as Fred Hirsch suggests, or by accident, perhaps by a sustained recession, it would become much less important for professors to dress well. In the meantime, perhaps the best that can be hoped for is that more academics will begin to analyze our society's cherished illusions about the relationship between education and the economy and the cash value of degrees, their own degrees as well as others'.

Andrew Levison in *The Working-Class Majority* has made a substantial start in this direction. He suggests that it is a serious mistake to imagine that most Americans are in white-collar job categories when, in fact, according to his estimates, some 60 percent work in blue-collar jobs. Describing his own experiences with the academic "yeah, yeah," he tells of one professor who criticized an early draft of his thesis "by first making a few disparaging remarks about statistics in general" and then observing that "there are workers in New York City's Department of Sanitation who earn as much as some City University of New York professors and more than Columbia assistant professors." This is the kind of assertion that infuriates Levison. It is "self-indulgent," he argues, to imagine that professors and other intellectuals suffer the same economic deprivation as the average worker; it is a "deeply destructive and pernicious" myth.

Unimpressed with the pain of disappointed ex-

pectation (being a professor means vacations in
Europe, a paneled library), he points to actual
income figures: "The average professor's salary
in 1970 was $11,745. . . . Operatives get on the
average $7,644 and craftsmen and foremen
$9,253. Even the lowly assistant professors re-
ceived more than skilled workers, $10,698 versus
$9,253. And even this does not show the magni-
tude of the error. This income of $11,745 in gen-
eral or $10,698 for assistant professors, includes a
three-month vacation. This is a nine-month work
year, one of the most popular features of a professor's job. If we compare weekly salaries to correct
for this difference, we find that professors average $293 a week. Full professors make, on the
average, a whopping $419 a week. The lowly as-
sistant professors make $265.

"The highest paid construction workers, the
skilled journeymen, got an average of $6.54 an
hour in 1970, or $262 a week.

"There it is. An assistant professor, who considers himself to be at the low end of the academic totem pole, averages more per hour than
the worker who has reached the very top of the
working-class hierarchy."[9]

Myths about underpayment prevail not because professors as a group mistrust statistics, but
because these myths are needed. They provide

[9] Andrew Levison, *The Working-Class Majority* (New York: Cow-
ard, McCann & Geoghegan, 1974), pp. 36–37.

THE SELF-PROJECTIVE CURRICULUM 119

psychic comfort. The image of the impoverished professor has a certain historical validity, but it is in larger part the product of envy—envy of other professionals. Most professors believe that physicians, for example, are egregiously overpaid, but it is less dangerous to whine about wealthy garbage men than to risk direct comparisons with doctors. An ironical "Can you believe that sanitation workers . . ." is a lot easier to come up with than a comparative analysis of the way various professional groups serve (and don't serve) the general good. Certainly it is pleasanter to think of oneself as underpaid and undervalued by a philistine world than to consider all the ways in which one's colleagues, through inattention and a certain amount of willful ignorance, have allowed the higher learning to become a commodity marketed like toothpaste or travel, with promises of improved social status and upward mobility, promises that in the end have more to do with the need of professors to think well of themselves than the reality of their students' lives.

"Hello, Jen?" the voice on the phone said, at two one morning. "It's Mel. Sorry to call you at home." Mel is the Acting Head of our department —Drama and Cinema. The Acting Head of the Acting Department, in a way. The Permanent Head, a flustered lady of pure steel, whose aca-

demic background consists of a Midwestern degree in Oral Science and a brief marriage to an
actor, is on a city grant to study Media History
abroad.

"Hi, Mel," I said to the Acting Head, as warmly
as I could.

"Jen, the Art Department wants to do a course
in Space on Film," he said. He paused. "We knew
you'd want to be informed." He paused again.
"And, without trying to influence you in any way,
we'd like to know what your position is." I
yawned. "Mel, I feel strongly about this," I said.
I had been teaching for some months. I was catch-
ing on. "I really do."

"We hoped you would," he said. "Len has just
pointed out—we're having coffee here—that
there are just two things on film. Time. And
Space. If we let the Art people go ahead with
Space, we'll have lost half . . ."

"Yes," I said. "And if the History Department
takes Time away . . ."

"Exactly." . . .

The Art people, then, met our people, regarding
Space. The meeting began quietly enough. "I particularly resent," Mel said, leafing to the fourth
page of a nine-page memorandum the Art people
had sent that morning, in reply to his own
eleven-page memorandum of the night before,
"your use of the word 'unconscionable.' It is inappropriate in a memoranda of this sort." . . .

Within three wrathful hours—in which, at one
point, our people understood the Art people to

have implied our people were unqualified to teach a course our people heard as Spaces, Gold-wyn-Giotto: Film and Fresca—we had resolved the question of Space on Film. It will be taught jointly, by our people and their people, in a semi-nar next spring. It will be listed under our people in the catalogue. If anything goes wrong, the featherbedding illiterates in our department will join the reactionary pedants in theirs to blame it on Open Admissions, . . . I won't be here next spring.[10]

[10] Renata Adler, *Speedboat* (New York: Random House, 1976), pp. 77–78, 81–82.

4

Presentation of Self: Selling Higher Education to the Public

BEARDSLEY RUML, who went from being dean of social sciences at the University of Chicago to become chairman of Macy's and of the Federal Reserve Bank of New York, believed that the curriculum was too important to be left to professors. "The individual members of the faculty are for the most part chosen as specialists in departmental subjects," he pointed out, "and as a result both of knowledge and personal interest each is a special advocate, necessarily and desirably so. A collection of special advocates cannot be expected to be a repository and a voice of judicial wisdom."[1]

"Bad as the quality of the liberal college curriculum" seemed to Ruml, however, he was convinced that other aspects of collegiate life had been even more shamefully neglected. In *Memo to a College Trustee* (1959), he suggested that the damage done by the poverty of academic institutions "is beyond all estimation. . . . To try to meet situations caused by financial inadequacy, administrative officers and glamour professors must be on call to impress officers of foundations, influential alumni, the rich potential donor, the corporation contributor with an eye on next year's recruiting program, and preparatory school sources for next year's tuition-paying students. And publicity, always publicity."[2]

Ruml's solutions for academic poverty, among them increasing the ratio of students to faculty members and of lectures to smaller classes, were never warmly embraced by the academic community. But he remained convinced that much "sectioning," dividing large lecture courses into smaller recitation classes, was a "make-work device" that encouraged a kind of interaction between teacher and student inappropriate at the college level. Seminars and tutorials might be ad-

---

[1] Beardsley Ruml, *Memo to a College Trustee: A Report on Financial and Structural Problems of the Liberal College* (New York: McGraw-Hill, 1959), p. 7.
[2] *Ibid.*, p. 8.

mirable things; the small lecture course was simply inefficient.

Anticipating a lack of enthusiasm on the part of the professors for his proposed reforms, Ruml insisted that the trustees "must take back from the faculty *as a body*, its present authority over the design and administration of the curriculum"[3] and in turn must create some new means of designing the academic program and determining the methods of instruction—perhaps a "New Council for Educational Policy and Program" to include faculty, administrators, and trustees.

Having tried to put Ruml's joint committee theory into practice at Bennington, I'm fairly sure it isn't the answer. Instead of helping faculty members to overcome a shortsighted sense of their own best interests, the establishment of a joint committee gave them something new to shoot at. They had almost no difficulty deciding that the professors on the committee were dupes or even traitors, eager to play along with the "big boys." And as for the nonfaculty members of the committee, well, they obviously didn't know much about education anyway.

When Bennington's most recent joint committee on future directions made its unpalatable recommendations (including adjusting student faculty ratio from 8:1 to 9.5:1) and the faculty

---

[3] *Ibid.*, p. 13.

refused to discuss any of them, one of my reactions was all right, let the faculty have it—the whole college. A reverse Ruml seemed in order. Instead of declaring the curriculum too important to be left to faculty members, the rest of the college's operations, from fundraising to maintenance, were clearly too important—and interconnected—to be left to anyone but faculty members. If they wished to proclaim themselves the college, fine. But then they should have responsibility for the whole damned thing.

One faculty member put the case in an open letter to Bennington's trustees:

> Newspapers are never accurate and they are often outrageous. There is ground for hoping, then, that the censure and disparagement of the . . . faculty ascribed . . . to [the chairman of the board] were never uttered—auditory illusions, perhaps created by the chill convexity of our northern morning air. Indeed, the more I consider it, the more certain I grow that the Chairman of our Board of Trustees could not have spoken so arrogantly or brandished her rights so menacingly. The trustees are said to love this college, and there is some evidence that they do. They could hardly at this moment, when wisdom must encourage them to consult their interests, be busy rehearsing their rights. The college is not what it is by virtue of trustees' rights; nor are students the spontaneous generation of those rights. The col-

lege does not derive its good name in the world from trustees' rights; nor is its merry personality the distillate of trustees' rights. That we faculty have been content to leave the world and be ill-paid for the privilege has nothing to do with trust-ees' rights. But it is the common-law of academies that trustees are given their rights so that they might bear a responsibility—of succor, or protec-tion and after all of deference—to the faculty and its natural authority.

I would agree that the trustee rights are irrele-vant in explaining why one college is more repu-table than another—not that faculty rights in and of themselves have much more to do with either generating students or good name. As for "merry personality," I know I found it hard to be sure that I had one myself when I read this diatribe for the first time. The general tone of the state-ment tempted me to go beyond fantasies of an-nouncing "the college is yours" to dream of sug-gesting what faculty members, at least some of them, could do with it.

Realists, policy experts, resource analysts, would argue that one cannot expect professors, involved in research and teaching, to devote time willingly much less ably to running the store. That is the business of specialists. I'm uncon-vinced. Obviously lawyers, brokers, accountants, and so forth need to be consulted. But there is every difference between an educational institution run by administrators with faculty members as employee/consultants, and one run by faculty members who consult expert managers. The point, I think, is not whether a notable academic becomes president or whether professors feel close to the administration, but whether faculty members can, indeed are required to, look at their particular institution as a whole instead of acting out the fable of the blind men with the elephant. Choices cannot be made, or made very well, by people who tend to mistake tails and toenails for the whole beast.

It is true that administrators have been known to conceal important information, trifling with those faculty members (and students) who ask to see the books. But there is blame enough to go around. In most cases administrative recalcitrance is the result of sad experience. Presidents, provosts, and deans quickly learn that the other so-called constituencies tend to trifle with them. Professors are eager to see budgets so that they can pick them apart. The tedious business of putting Humpty together again is not for them.

And whatever the intermittent appeal of establishing faculty budget committees, there is rarely commensurate interest in scrutinizing the college or university's presentation of self. Few professors have ever bothered to study fundraising brochures or the four-color viewbooks sent out to prospective students. It's understandable. These

publications are enough to stir the Bartleby response in anyone concerned about the future of
the higher learning. Would you read this? I
would prefer not to.

Of course today you don't have to be able to
read to get the message. Academic public relations journals currently advocate using records,
flexible plastic discs that can be stapled into mag-
azines, making it possible for prospective students and donors to "hear the sounds of the campus." Homecoming rallies, student loyalists—
"Here at ———— 57 percent of the faculty have
Ph.D.s; they really challenge you to think,"
chapel bells, all the background music of happy
college days.

One of the most important of these public relations journals, *Currents,* is published by the
Council for the Advancement and Support of Education. Reading through the "great ideas" outlined in this magazine, it is hard to escape the
conclusion that prime time television has become
the source of cultural allusions and images at a
number of American colleges. Whatever role
Aristotle may continue to play at the University
of Chicago, at many academic institutions he has
been upstaged by characters drawn from commercials, game shows, and situation comedies.

Findlay College's recruitment package, for example, is based on the theme "It's great to be a
big fish in a small college" and features a poster

"with a note hanging down 'Charley Tuna style.' " Viterbo College links its message with the media by sponsoring "High Quiz Bowl," a weekly television program involving high school students. The prizes are Viterbo scholarships. There are no losers. Donnelly College's promotional literature is apparently a spinoff from "Happy Days." "Donnelly's Got a Great Rep" is the title of their recruitment folder which is written in "1950's hip style" and is "a hit."

There are twenty-two more "great ideas" where these came from—a single issue of *Currents*. But to pile example on example is to risk burying the point. It's not that these glossy posters and television shows and brochures are commercial and therefore bad, it is that they are bad commercials. They may attract attention and even increase enrollment temporarily, but unlike truly successful advertising campaigns, they create such misleading expectations about the nature of the product that over the long run they can only undermine public confidence. Charley the Tuna was created to suggest that some tuna packers are more discriminating than others. The message that Charley or any of his ilk, conveys about higher education is far less complimentary.

Reading through these great ideas is enough to make me believe that Cardinal Newman's warning "On the Scope and Nature of University Education" (1854) should be carved into every admissions officer's desk: "Do not say that people must be educated when after all you only mean amused, refreshed, soothed, put into good spirits and good humor, or kept from vicious excess." After all, publicity is not sent out from the college or university never to be seen again. Lyndon Johnson's preference for having someone inside his tent pissing out rather than outside pissing in represents an option educational institutions don't have. Some of what is directed at the outside world comes back—in the form of expectations—and student expectations are a crucial part of the educational experience. Lured by Charley the Tuna, a "college bowl-type" media event, or a booklet written in the native tongue of the Fonz, anyone might reasonably expect that going to college will be as much keen fun as four years of prime time television.

Advertising as such has been a feature of American academic life for more than a century. In the 1800s many more colleges went bankrupt than survived, and the survivors were willing to try almost anything to achieve the elusive goal of having "enough" students. In 1871–72, the last year of Mark Hopkins's presidency at Williams, the college had 119 students. It had 119 students when he had taken office thirty-five years before. At the time of Hopkins's retirement, a speaker at the Boston alumni association suggested that Williams might benefit from an advertising campaign in the nation's press. As it so happened, the campaign had already been launched.

In 1904 Dean Albion W. Small designed a circular to be distributed to seniors at "leading colleges" inviting them to attend graduate school at the University of Chicago. The billboard outside O'Hare Airport advertising a lesser-known Midwestern institution is, in one sense, as traditional as dormitories with Georgian and Gothic facades. There is an important difference, of course, between announcing the existence of a course of study at a given institution and suggesting in the pages of *The New York Times* that if you "Fly Adelphi" you can "Get Where You Want to Go in Life." But the switch from advertising the availability of a product to insinuating that the buyer will gain in panache has less to do with changes in the "ed biz" than in the art of advertising. In 1900 most advertisers, not just the University of Chicago, were satisfied to describe what they had to sell. Subsequently the proliferation of consumer goods and the development of national markets (for colleges as well as cornflakes) made it necessary to hint at connections between patterns of consumption and life-style.

The "Fly Adelphis" and travesties celebrated in *Currents* represent the imposition of an alien aesthetic on the academic world. Yet just as it would be naive to imagine that the military-in-

dustrial complex seduced virginal professors (or
students) into supporting the Vietnam War or
going to work for Chase Manhattan, it would be
foolish to think that the advertising industry is
guilty of leading academic innocents astray. They
go willingly.

Professor Kenneth Dolbeau, in a bitter analysis
of faculty power, has suggested "that faculty government is often mere co-optation. Even its most
vigorous and sincere celebrants acknowledge
that it carries with it the corollary principle of
faculty responsibility. The latter often simply
amounts to doing what one thinks the Regents
would do before they have a chance to do it. In
order to preserve one's independence, in other
words, one acts as one anticipates one's superiors
would prefer."[4]

This readiness to salute is not what I mean to
encourage by talking about the obligations faculty members have if they *are* in fact the college
or university. Nor am I at all sure that it is a readiness that regents and trustees would encourage.
Implicit in Dolbeau's what "one's superiors
would prefer" is a paramilitary hierarchy where
the junior officers are expected to model themselves after the chicken colonels and brigadiers.
But in my experience, while trustees have little

[4] Kenneth M. Dolbeau, "Faculty Power," in *Academic Supermarkets*, Philip G. Altbach, Robert S. Lauter, Sheila McVey, eds. (San
Francisco: Jossey-Bass, 1971), p. 165.

fondness for insurrections and insurrectionaries, they are not particularly eager to listen to faculty members' impersonations of trustees. If anything, they want to feel that they are hearing "the other side," that they are in touch with values other than those of the bottom line; that's part of the pleasure of being a board member.

In fact the notion that a "responsible" faculty member is necessarily a trustee manqué probably has more to do with the professors' need to believe that they are as hard-nosed as any lawyer or businessman than with the wishes of the lawyers and businessmen themselves. William James used to torment his younger brother Henry with the taunt that *he* played with boys who cursed and swore. There is a certain academic chic about playing with the big boys, perhaps an attempt to make up for early bookishness, shyness, shortness, whatever.

A good example of this compensatory behavior can be drawn from the coeducation debates at previously all-male colleges and universities. Surprisingly large numbers of faculty members preened themselves during those debates on their superior "realism," that is, their ability to anticipate the thinking of "big givers." Everyone knew, according to these savants, that women don't earn as much as men and when they do are less likely to give generously to their alma maters. Therefore coeducation would hurt future alumni giving as well as disturb many current donors.

The possibility that times were changing, that some women actually might be more financially successful than their male classmates and more inclined to support an institution that opened its doors to them, was rarely mentioned in faculty discussions. The debate over coeducation gave the male professors an opportunity to confirm their chosen self-images: saintly liberals welcoming the disadvantaged (into student ranks if not their own), or men of the world, resolute in the face of any threat to their paychecks or perquisites.

Questioned individually, almost any professor will be sharply critical of the level of debate in departmental conclaves or faculty meetings. Taken one by one they sound more like latter-day Catharine Esther Beechers than boosters or lobbyists. But despite individual scruples, as a group they often seem to prefer pseudo-discussions and pseudo-events to the real thing.

"Pseudo-events" have been usefully defined by the historian Daniel Boorstin as events planned, planted, or excited primarily for the purpose of being reported or reproduced. The relationship of the pseudo-event to the underlying reality of a given situation is always ambiguous. When one sees how a stereotype has been produced and discovers the sources of propaganda, that stereotype becomes less believable. This, says Boorstin, is not the case with a pseudo-event, for information about how it was staged simply adds to the fascination.[5]

Far more seductive then than stereotypes, pseudo-events can often overshadow real events. They are intentionally dramatic. They can be repeated at will. They cost money and therefore are advertised in advance to ensure a return on investment. Having been designed for intelligibility they are more intelligible, and hence more reassuring than the real thing. Today, according to Boorstin, a knowledge of pseudo-events is *the* test of being informed. The common discourse which some of his "old fashioned friends have hoped to find in the Great Books" is now provided by carefully managed and packaged "news."[6]

Curriculum reform in the last two or three years has been transformed from a sporting event into a pseudo-event. Although the pervasive sense of choices not made can be counted on in academic communities to create interest in almost any debatable topic, the real source of the curriculum reform impulse today is not spontaneous dissatisfaction. The discussions are excited, one might say fomented, by deans of faculty, presidents, and politically ambitious faculty

[5] Daniel J. Boorstin, *The Image: Or What Happened to the American Dream?* (New York: Atheneum, 1962), pp. 11–12, 38.
[6] *Ibid.*, pp. 38–40.

members whose idea of behaving responsibly involves anticipating the wishes of supposed higher-ups.

Shortly before a straw vote was taken on proposed curriculum changes last spring, the president of one particularly prestigious college, according to the student newspaper, "addressed the implications of the upcoming formal vote on the capital fund drive and ———'s national image. [He] made a plea that the faculty approve *some* form of curricular revision, citing outside expectations that ——— will be among the leaders in the nationwide search for an effective liberal arts curriculum.

"[He] also feared that a final vote to maintain ———'s curricular status quo would seriously harm the major capital campaign. The lack of a coherent curriculum, he said, might impair the 'ability of people to say they will support a first class place.' "

It is probably better not to try to reproduce faculty discussions verbatim if one is interested in intelligibility. But bits and pieces, agendas, progress reports, can and are produced today for the sole purpose of being reported. The relationship between a pseudo-curriculum discussion and the actual business of education is decidedly ambiguous. And although it is tempting to think of a curriculum resembling all other curricula as a species of stereotype, what has in fact been produced on most campuses is a true pseudo-event according to Boorstin's definition, for great pleasure is taken by participants and their audience (alumni, trustees, parents) in discovering just how the whole thing was staged.

At the college where the president openly feared it would look bad not to have some sort of curriculum reforms, the faculty committee that came up with the specific proposals regaled trustees with an after-dinner account of "how we pulled it off." The drama of who said what to whom and how political disaster was averted was clearly far more intriguing than the "real" event, the inevitable report recommending that core courses be reestablished.

It is possible to think of curriculum reform as the moral equivalent of the after-dinner speech, nothing to get upset about, unless one has an urgent sense of alternative agendas. Perhaps the same people who have permitted Charley the Tuna to speak on behalf of the collegiate experience had best be kept in good spirits and away from vicious excess.

Yet the thought that professors, people with unusual resources of money, time, and training at their disposal, are unable to tell the difference between a publicity stunt and a watershed in the history of the mind is genuinely horrifying. Willing to have stock in their joint enterprise sold to the public via prospectuses that bear no resemblance to their own understanding of the business, unconcerned about the morality—to say nothing of the waste—involved in raising false expectations about a college education . . . it is this professorial refusal to take responsibility, *not* the inanities uttered on their behalf by hired flacks, that is at the heart of current disenchantment with higher education. And the only way to restore faith is not by puns on value and values, but by faculty members' asserting their natural authority and refusing to let other people lie on their behalf.

Andrew Levison's suggestion that the white-collar majority is a convenient fiction has clear implications for higher education. The apologists who would argue that the size and public expense of the existing educational establishment is justified because it and it alone guarantees upward mobility for all ambitious Americans, sooner or later should find Levison's analysis sobering. And recently, the primary rationale for credentialism—that the educated employee is in fact a better employee—has been seriously undermined by research.

"To argue that well-educated people will automatically boost efficiency, improve organizations, and so on may be to misunderstand in a fundamental way the nature of American education, which functions to an important, indeed depressing extent as a licensing agency.

"A search of the considerable literature on productivity, absenteeism, and turnover has yielded little concrete evidence of a positive relationship between workers' educational achievements and their performance records in many work settings in the private sector."[7]

The news gets worse. Not only is there scant evidence that education makes for efficiency, there is little reason to believe that specific skills presumed to be acquired by an undergraduate degree are relevant to most people's work experience. According to James O'Toole in "The Reserve Army of the Unemployed," the Bureau of Labor Statistics has estimated that only about 20 percent of all jobs will require a college education for successful performance in 1980. The Office of Management and Budget has found that one-half of all current jobs do not even require a high-school education."[8]

A less statistical, more philosophical kind of investigation would suggest that perhaps the clearest "success" of American higher education has been to teach students that they have only themselves to blame when they finally enter the job market and find that there just aren't enough good (positional) jobs to go around. In 1968, Christopher Jencks and David Riesman described how

[7] Ivar Berg, *Education and Jobs: The Great Training Robbery* (New York: Praeger, 1970), p. 104.
[8] James O'Toole, "The Reserve Army of the Unemployed," *Change*, May 1975, p. 32.

colleges function to "cool out" young men and women whose ambitions and ability go unrewarded, while managing to preserve the appearance of fairness to all.

Building on Jencks and Riesman's analysis, Richard Sennett and Jonathan Cobb (*The Hidden Injuries of Class*) have been even more condemnatory of the function of the higher learning. Like Jencks and Riesman they believe that working-class students are made to feel inadequate by a "laying on of culture" practiced by their teachers and more privileged classmates, and as a consequence these students become convinced that their dissatisfactions, even before graduation, are the result of character flaws: "I still don't have the balls to go out into the world." "If I really had what it takes, I could make this school thing worthwhile."[9]

Potentially a means to greater freedom, education, according to Sennett and Cobb, has become a major "source of indignity." ". . . The frustration and resentment threatened by the gap between promised reward and continued constraint of freedom is diverted into a problem of the self, so that even as the young college-educated [shoe salesman] . . . feels angry about what has happened in his life, his anger at the 'System' is undercut because inwardly he also blames

[9] Richard Sennett and Jonathan Cobb, *The Hidden Injuries of Class* (New York: Alfred A. Knopf, 1973), p. 27.

himself for not making something of his opportunities." [10]

What the work of these sociologists suggests is that professors, by combining a priestly respect for texts with a studied disregard for the effects of false promises, have managed to do the dirty work of American society in ways far subtler than the foes of either "the system" or of a narrow-minded vocationalism have ever suggested. It is not so much that faculty members train youths to fit in; indeed, there is ample evidence that education and occupational fit are poorly correlated at best. It is that they teach their students in countless ways to believe that when they don't find an appropriate slot, don't have the kind of career that the publicists for higher education have led them to expect, they have only themselves to blame.

I realize that it may seem inconsistent to suggest that students should *not* be taught to feel that personal inadequacies alone keep them from flying Adelphi or any other university to the career of their dreams, while arguing that professors should assume greater personal responsibility for their lives. I confess to a double standard. For if education in any sense means freedom, an increased range of options and a greater ability to distinguish among them, then it is only fair to

[10] *Ibid.*, p. 180.

expect that teachers assume greater responsibility for their choices than their students, while
doing everything possible to help those students
assume the same burden of freedom.

Sennett and Cobb have a good deal to say about
the American tendency to romanticize professional life and think of doctors and lawyers and
professors as people who don't have to separate
their deepest selves from the self that goes to
work in the morning. This may be romantic, but
it has a certain truth. Or it should. On soap operas
nine out of ten men are professionals. Most of the
rest are hoodlums. Why? Because these are the
two groups of people who are believed to have
the freedom to express themselves on the job and
who therefore have working lives that can be dra-
matized in broadly human terms.

It is tempting to think that professors have not
made it as soap opera heroes because they are
perceived, if only dimly, as the professionals who
put nonprofessionals in their place. They are the
credentialers, the ones who lay on culture instead
of easing your pain like the kindly doctor, or defending you like the TV lawyer. Small wonder
that conversations between faculty adviser and
student are not the stuff of midday dreams.

Of course any professional commitment may be
an elaborate way of avoiding self-knowledge, of
substituting careerism for a close look at one's
own priorities. The assistant professors produc-

ing articles on button imagery in Chaucer cannot be thought of as entirely free agents, at least not if we are to maintain our respect for them as human beings. The importance of finding a safe orthodoxy and job niche, of making the right moves, severely limits the ability of the professional academic to do more than try to score a few "yeah, yeahs" against the competition.

Yet if there is anything truly valuable about higher degrees (and positional jobs), it must be that they offer an opportunity to speak your mind while requiring that you know what you're talking about. Unfortunately, professors, while insisting that they play a crucial role in preserving and propagating culture, have up until now been content to let others manage the difficult business of explaining their mission to a skeptical world. At most they have been willing to participate in a ceremonial laying on of hands. It is easy enough to find it mildly ridiculous for a cardinal to give his blessing to the World Series; the professor of philosophy or literature paid by the National Endowment of the Humanities to bring his learned allusions to bear on community debate over care for the elderly, atomic power, or pollution at the local reservoir, generally seems just about as silly.

But worse than any silliness is the way in which academics have failed to defend the intellectual freedom of their fellows, first by merely

tolerating and now by playing an increasingly active role in efforts to promote a superstitious faith
in the higher learning. For years they have done
little to ensure that the public is informed, as opposed to propagandized, about the value of
higher education. And more recently, by cooper-
ating in the production of pseudo-events, college
bowl-type games and carefully stage-managed
curriculum reforms, they have been actively implicated in disingenuous attempts to manipulate
public opinion.

Even now when the claims of higher education
sound increasingly shrill and it is apparent that a
bachelor's degree can no longer be marketed as a
guarantee of the good life, how many professors
are heard expressing remorse for having failed to
look into their own advertising? Traditionally a
sense of superiority has kept them from taking
their messages to the public—someone without
anything better to do, an administrator, could always be found to confuse the issues of value and
values for them. Now they feel betrayed. Why
should their jobs be jeopardized because a
twenty-five-year-old publicity campaign finally
backfired? *They* never said that taking their
courses would enable students to "gt gd jb mo
py."

Yet the professors rarely, very rarely, said,
"Wait a minute, I'm not sure about that. I don't
think we have enough evidence. What is the ac-

tual relationship of jobs and degrees? What should it be?" The historical coincidence of high postwar birthrate and dramatic growth in the white-collar sector of the job market is over now, but it remains to be seen whether the professors have learned much about the long-term dangers of convenient myths. So far there seems to have been little professorial resistance to a national ad campaign for values that seems designed to give the "Great Conversation" a talk-show format.

Universities, it is said, are about "excellence." The abstraction is apt, but such universal evocations of quality need interpretation that they not become shibboleth savants. Particular clarification is required as the UHP asserts its transcendent concern with one dimension of academic excellence: the educational dimension as applied to the capable and achievement oriented undergraduate student. Specifically, we are in the business of providing challenging educational opportunities for qualified students who seek both breadth and depth in their collegiate studies. Our concern with excellence is to make visceral a conception of quality for these students through demanding and stimulating curricular offerings, including independent study, in combination with reasonable expectations for student attainment. It seems evident that substantiating these aspirations for quality will be an evolving process as we nourish inchoate ambitions into a steady-state program. It also seems clear the Program will bear the mark of departments and individual faculty who choose to participate in establishing a program to engender honors caliber work at Pitt. May we interest you in having an affair with quality?—*Letter from the director of the University of Pittsburgh Honors Program.*

Well, not in those exact words.[11]

[11] *The New Yorker*, April 13, 1978.

5

Preservation of Self: Tenure

THERE IS perverse pleasure in the thought that those who write soap operas were quicker than sociologists to sense that no matter how warmly human individual professors may be, as a group they are paid to put other people in their places. Whether they spend every afternoon advising students or limit their "contact hours" to bi-weekly lectures, in the end it makes relatively little difference—it is the professors' business to categorize, not console. And any uneasiness that they might feel about performing this function is minimized by their unconscious assumption that because they are discriminating among ideas they are qualified to discriminate between persons.

There is a kind of paradox here: on the one hand academics don't worry about serving a screening function in the economy because they don't think of their choices in that context; on the other, they imagine that if anyone has to perform that function they're the logical ones to do so. Actually this is more a quandary than a paradox, and a fairly common quandary at that. We all at one time or another have gotten through difficult situations by trying to imagine the situation didn't exist, while at the same time telling ourselves that if anyone could handle it we could. Willed ignorance is different from pure ignorance; it always has an admixture of knowing better. And in trying to understand how academics could allow themselves to be used as credentialers, we should assume that although they would rather not know what they are doing, they do know, and have already justified their behavior in their own minds.

In truth the same ahistoricism that enables professors and presidents and deans to imagine that curriculum debates are somehow "about" the eternal verities makes them more preoccupied than the average person with questions of status. If there are Values, Truths that exist out of time and out of context, then those who understand them are obviously a higher order of being than those who don't. At the heart of all the gabble about quality and excellence is a fundamentally aristocratic perspective on life, and it is this perspective that finally reconciles professors to playing the role of credentialer.

As Howard Mumford Jones has observed,

> The academic hierarchy from teaching fellows up through the august body of full professors is something we commonly discuss in terms of rank —a word we also use about aristocratic society. It is not too fantastic to say that tenure implies aristocratic privilege—privilege not too unlike the privilege of a nobility—and academic nobility has the power, and alone has the power, to recruit its numbers through a scale of ceremonies signifying a scale of degrees, culminating through higher degrees in any case of special distinction in something called an honorary degree. The ceremonial of commencement is intended to impress onlookers with the validity of our aristocratic values, partly social, partly intellectual; and I think it significant that on court occasions we of the academic world invariably break out our ceremonial robes and hoods and gold tassels, marching not higgledy-piggledy or in alphabetical order, but in due academic dignity.[1]

Jones's observations are more picturesque than the official pronouncements of the American As-

[1] Howard Mumford Jones, "The American Concept of Academic Freedom," *The American Scholar*, Winter 1959–60, p. 234.

sociation of University Professors, but both point essentially the same moral. Spokesmen for the AAUP are always careful to say that "the demand we of the academic world make for academic freedom is not made primarily for our own benefit. We enjoy the exercise of freedom; but the purposes of liberty lie, in a democracy, in the common welfare."[2]

There is no reason to believe that statements like these are cynical in intention, designed simply to placate the lowbrows. My own impression is that the men who have written them over the years sincerely believe that academic freedom is crucial to the preservation of democracy, and they are almost certainly right. But there is a great deal of difference between saying that the ultimate "purpose" of your freedoms is the common welfare, and commiting yourself to make active use of them to ensure the freedom of your fellow man.

The expressions of concern about the common welfare in AAUP manifestos are generally qualified by subsequent sentences that establish a sense of distance between academics and ordinary folk. The demurrer about not demanding academic freedom "primarily for our own benefit," for example, is followed by a statement describ-

[2] American Association of University Professors, 1956 report on "Relevant General Principles," Louis Joughin, *Academic Freedom and Tenure: A Handbook of the American Association of University Professors* (Madison: University of Wisconsin Press, 1967), p. 48.

ing the gulf between what professors feel they need and what they think is necessary for their neighbors. "The occupational work of the vast majority of people is largely independent of their thought and speech. The professor's work consists of his thought and speech."[3] And therefore, or so the AAUP logic goes, the professors need special protections.

The smugness of the official literature of the American Association of University Professors reflects that group's aristocratic predilections, but it is not untypical of the pronouncements of those associations made up of other professionals. Professionals generally differ from nonprofessionals in their overriding concern for collegial repute, their standing in the eyes of their peers. The individual who pushes Laetrile or curries student favor, in other words, who looks to customer satisfaction as a primary measure of success, is dismissed by his colleagues as a quack. In academic circles this professional orientation reinforces the idea that research done with, and primarily for, one's colleagues is a worthier activity than teaching, and exacerbates the tendency to regard the whole business of academic public relations as beneath professorial notice.

The core curriculum enthusiasts would have us believe that professionalization is something new

[3] *Ibid.*, p. 48.

in academic life; that professors have traditionally been interested in, and capable of, molding
character. Yet as early as 1902, Bliss Perry wrote
in the *Atlantic Monthly* that a "newer type of
college professor" is "everywhere in evidence":

> the expert who knows all about railroads and
> bridges and subways; about gas commissioners
> and electrical supplies; about currency and banks,
> Philippine tariffs, Venezuelan boundary lines, the
> industries of Puerto Rico, the classification of the
> civil service, the control of trusts. . . . The college
> professor who represents the "humanities," rather
> than the distinctly scientific side of modern edu-
> cation, is likewise brought closer to the public
> than ever before. The newspapers report—and
> mis-report—him. Editors offer him space to reply.
> Publishers weary him with appeals to write text
> books . . . The professor's photograph . . . assaults
> your eye in the marketplace. The college press
> club and the university's bureau of publicity give
> his lecture dates in advance. The prospectus of
> your favorite magazine bids you inspect his liter-
> ary qualifications as well as his thoughtful coun-
> tenance. *Who's Who in America* informs you of
> the name of his second wife.[4]

Whatever the drawbacks of this self-promoting
professionalism, only the most blindly nostalgic
could conclude that academic life was purer and

[4] Bliss Perry, "College Professors and the Public," *Atlantic
Monthly*, March 1902, pp. 284–85.

nobler in the good old days when, as one ob-
server wrote in 1871, the American professor "is
too often only a nondescript, a jack of all trades,
equally ready to teach surveying as Latin elo-
quence, and thankful if his quarter's salary is not
docked to whitewash the college fence."[5] Even
the most notable of the old-style professors, men
like Mark Hopkins who was reputedly a liberal
education in himself, seem doubtful models in
retrospect. Hopkins, for example, was once
known to boast, "I don't read any books; in fact I
never did read any books."[6]

Those today who argue for a resurrection of the
professor/mentor presumably don't mean to encourage anti-intellectualism, but they have been
able to argue that it makes sense for faculty members whose entire training and professional orientation has been marked by a high degree of
specialization to teach broadly conceived courses
on man, nature, and values, because of the pervasive confusion of professionalism and mandarinism in American academic life. Both sets of
values encourage a sense of separateness—and
superiority—yet it would be hard to find two
ways of thinking about one's place in the world
that are more at odds. The mandarin (or academic
aristocrat) believes himself superior to nonaca-

[5] Anonymous, "The Higher Education in America," *Galaxy*, March
1871, p. 373.
[6] Frederick Rudolph, *Mark Hopkins and the Log* (New Haven: Yale
University Press, 1956), p. 77.

demics because he has a special relationship to certain timeless truths—the Wisdom of Aristotle, the Scientific Method—while the professional rests his case on the fact that he has specific information and expert skills.

There is probably no better illustration of the rationalizing power of the academic mind than the ease with which professors move back and forth between mandarinism and professionalism in defending their claims to a privileged place in society. Over twenty years ago when Russian technology seemed to pose the greatest single threat to the American way of life, academics encouraged the notion that they were the specialists, the experts, the only ones who could save the nation. Now that the Vietnam debacle and Watergate have created a widespread sense of moral disarray, they have begun to promote the idea that they are the priests, the Brahmins, the last best hope for teaching young Americans something about values.

On balance, the scientifically oriented are more likely to adhere to a strictly professional code—humanists go in for rank. They tend to sound like dispossessed Czech princes or remnants of the czar's imperial guard when they talk about declining enrollments. Their esoteric knowledge *should* give them special status. And if colleagues in the more popular disciplines were not such vulgarians they would restore the crown of "requirement" to history and foreign languages and literature.

Still, no matter how much the failure to distinguish between professionalism and mandarinism has muddled curriculum debate, it has had an even more destructive effect on discussions of the faculty contract system. Tenure, as Howard Mumford Jones points out, "implies aristocratic privilege," and yet the spokesmen for the academic profession often prefer to argue that tenure is really just like the agreements between partners in a law firm or physicians with joint hospital privileges—a way of expressing broad collegial obligations in contractual terms.

Their line of defense varies depending on the nature of the attack. When professors are accused of wanting special privileges they argue that they're only interested in protecting the right of professionals to judge their fellow professionals. In this context the crucial feature of the tenure system is the rigorous process of scrutiny that each would-be professor must undergo. Yet when they are criticized for not keeping up that scrutiny once tenure has been granted, they insist on separating themselves not only from nonprofessionals but from doctors and lawyers, indeed anyone who does not understand that the life of the mind is an ineffable thing that cannot be subject to regular review.

In his presidential address to the Fiftieth Annual Meeting of the American Association of University Professors (April 10, 1964), Fritz Machlup spoke movingly "In Defense of Academic Tenure." The drawbacks, he admitted, were real. Tenure might protect "deadwood" and demoralize those professors who needed a constant spur. "Up or out" decisions were cruel and unfair in some cases. The process of "upgrading" the faculty in a department or college was made much more difficult. Tenure might even depress salaries by restricting the mobility of senior faculty members, thereby limiting their bargaining power. But all these disadvantages were, in Machlup's mind, outweighed by a single great advantage, "really the only justification for the system of academic tenure"—academic freedom.

As Machlup described him, the ideal professor would be "uninhibited" in his willingness to criticize and advocate changes in

"(1) accepted theories,
(2) widely held beliefs,
(3) existing social, political, and economic institutions,
(4) the policies and programs of the educational institution at which he serves, and
(5) the administration and governing board of the institution at which he serves.
(6) In addition, we want him to be unin-

hibited in coming to the aid of any of his colleagues whose academic freedom is in jeopardy."[7]

If only more professors had tenure it would be a better world. But then, in a manner reminiscent of Hofstadter describing the way antebellum academics actually behaved (as opposed to the way they *might* have behaved), Machlup struck a note of sober realism: "It is not necessary to assume that there are several Galileos in every generation or several men who have similarly subversive ideas of similar importance to communicate. The case for tenure would be sufficiently supported by showing that a few men once in a while might feel insecure and suppress or postpone the communication of views which, true or false, wise or foolish, could inspire or provoke others to embark on or continue along lines of reasoning which may eventually lead to new insights, new judgments, or new appraisals regarding nature or society."[8]

I cannot help feeling that if the best you can hope for is a chance that being heavily armored will make a marginal difference, the whole elaborate apparatus of tenure is a monument to the lack of perspective that characterizes so much academic thought. Surely grown men (and the women Machlup leaves out) would be more em-

[7] Joughin, *op. cit.*, p. 328
[8] *Ibid.*, p. 337.

barrassed than heartened by the idea that such great precautions were necessary to protect such small potential gains. But in fact the real significance of tenure from the professorial point of view is not the greater good, any more than that is the real significance of academic freedom. Academic freedom and the tenure that protects it may promote the general welfare in some abstract way. What is of more immediate importance to most academics, however, is that these particular claims are ways of asserting their right, or what they see as their right, to enjoy special privileges. And they will use any convenient argument, whether based on mandarin or professional assumptions, to protect these privileges.

In the long run it is this kind of intellectual legerdemain and not the attacks of outsiders that will bring about the destruction of the tenure system—unless, of course, academics are willing to rethink their assumptions first. As Nicholas Von Hoffman puts it, "Professors have been caught manipulating the game too often."

Most nonacademics, Von Hoffman included, would read Machlup's arguments for tenure as a confession of weakness, but to many professors they sound more like a celebration of potency. We need tenure, or so the implicit reasoning goes, because we are dangerous to society. We say things—like Miles in James's *Turn of the Screw*—unmentionable things that would surely get us thrown out of school unless we had special, special protection.

Over the years there have been disgraceful examples of trustees and legislators and administrators trampling on the rights of professors, professors who were challenging shibboleths in just the ways Machlup would applaud. But there have been other cases, unrecorded in the annals of the AAUP, in which faculty members were driven from their posts by inside rather than outside pressures to conform. The instances when uncomfortable colleagues are not promoted because of the prejudices and pettiness of their peers are rarely documented, although in some cases individuals have been hounded from tenured positions.

During the last century, for example, a venerable Union College professor named John Foster refused to support a faculty *putsch* against the president. In the course of the controversy he received a note from a young colleague which announced, "If I did not join them, I would certainly be destroyed," a threat that was carried out as soon as the president had been unseated. One of Foster's former students, who was now a professor, reported to the trustees that Foster neglected his teaching duties and taught outmoded interpretations of physics. (After forty-seven years at Union there may well have been substantial truth to the charges.) A secret letter was cir-

culated among the faculty seeking to prove that
Foster had originally been willing to sign a petition against the president and then had betrayed
his promise. Within six months the trustees declared that "the long and useful services of Prof.
John Foster L.L.D. entitle him to be exempted
from the burdens of his professorship."[9]

Sidney Hook, the academic philosopher, has
described a more recent case of faculty intolerance, an effort to "deprive" a Brooklyn College
professor "of his livelihood." According to Hook,
with that flair for reasoning by analogy that makes
me uneasy about many of his assertions, Bertrand
Russell himself would have been declared "unfit
to teach" at Brooklyn College because he exe-
cuted secret commissions in 1950 for the British
Foreign Office.

Apparently a majority of the members of the
political science department at Brooklyn (tipped
off by the professor's brother-in-law—can soap
opera be far behind?) concluded that because
their colleague had talked to someone in the Central Intelligence Agency about his experiences
abroad he was "guilty of unprofessional conduct
warranting dismissal." They alleged that his "behavior violates his professional responsibility,
since he has become privy to secrets that he can-

[9] George E. Peterson, *The New England College in the Age of the
University* (Amherst, Mass.: Amherst College Press, 1964), pp. 140–
41.

not discuss with colleagues and students. And so in the name of academic freedom," Hook observes mordantly, "the professor is to be deprived of his academic freedom." [10]

Whatever the facts may be in this particular case, it is not hard for me to imagine instances where a professor's cooperation with the CIA would be a wholly legitimate matter for professional censure. But it seems necessary to recognize the difference between cooperation and co-optation, between sharing information and sharing secrets in a way that would render an individual incapable of revealing either her data or assumptions in an intellectually responsible manner. This distinction has not always been made in the current debate about faculty codes of ethics because the professors' motives in pursuing these discussions are mixed. On the one hand they are deeply concerned about intellectual integrity—on the other they are indulging in a certain amount of preening: "We are so interesting that everyone, even the CIA, would like to be in on our secrets; we are so pure that we resist all offers—in advance." The professor as perpetual virgin.

In the end, whatever questions might be raised by a particular case, it is as illegitimate to define "academic freedom" in terms of majority opinion

[10] Sidney Hook, "To Teach the Truth, Without Let or Hindrance," *The Chronicle of Higher Education*, April 4, 1977.

in a given department or university as it is to embrace the myth of academic neutrality as a cover for dissident activity. Nothing shows the academics' contempt for nonacademics more clearly than these attempts to make arguments of convenience sound like rallying cries for all the friends of freedom. In the long run no one is fooled; in the short run academics have done a fair job of outsmarting themselves.

By defending tenure in terms of academic freedom, for example, professors have made it almost impossible to analyze just how tenure actually functions. Yet this kind of analysis is exactly what they need if they are to "be" the college or university in anything other than a ceremonial sense. Machlup's list of drawbacks could have been the first part of an examination of whether the current contract system helps or hurts professors, but he cut off further thinking by waving the flag and proclaiming tenure indispensable if the world is to be kept safe for democracy.

Machlup's paeans are in marked contrast to the recent observations of Peter Drucker, a management consultant as well as an academic, who believes that tenure is a "self-defeating" policy that entraps professors, ensuring that fewer and fewer new faculty members will be hired and that therefore fewer and fewer students will go on to graduate school, which in turn will further reduce the number of job openings in higher education. Drucker is convinced that as the pressures to cut faculty size and salaries increase, colleges are in real danger of becoming "the railroads of the knowledge industry."[11]

In his analysis these trends can only be reversed by combining systematic personnel development, including placement of the middle-aged "average" professor in work outside academe, with a system of renewable contracts. These contracts (one of the least palatable parts of the joint committee report on Bennington College's future) should be awarded only after careful review, not only by immediate colleagues but by professors from other institutions and "probably" also laymen, "particularly alumni." In Drucker's opinion, unless these reforms are made, college and university faculty members will become "just 'employees'—junior-high-school teachers with inflated degrees and deflated pay—in their standing, their self-respect, their influence, and their role in society."

Drucker had the temerity to summarize his thoughts in *The Chronicle of Higher Education,* the official organ of the education establishment. If the letters published in response are representative, the establishment was not amused.

What Drucker fails to recognize is that his draconian solution would destroy scholars' *freedom* to be exciting by seeking the truth and reporting

[11] Peter Drucker, "The Professor as Featherbedder," *The Chronicle of Higher Education,* January 31, 1977.

what they have found. Without this freedom the scholars can scarcely be expected to be excited about either teaching or research. Without freedom they can be replaced by clerks or teaching machines.

Russell L. Berry,
Economics Department,
South Dakota State University

Of all people, Professor Drucker should know that by comparison with the business executives he advises, college professors make a pittance, subsidizing the very institutions within which they labor. In what other area of life do people spend so many years preparing themselves for their work and then selflessly dedicate themselves to the common good? Given such conditions, why should we turn on our colleagues in midstream and say there is no longer room in the boat? We simply need a larger ship.

Louis Wildman, President,
Institute for
Quality in Human Life

Join me, skeptical colleagues, in accepting Dr. Drucker's assurances that within 12 months you shall, as I will be, miraculously rejuvenated, lecturing each morning to enthusiastic students, and publishing each afternoon in some "Sun-Belt" academic workers' commune. Shame on you of little faith who demand evidence of this outcome! Ask me *not*, for I pawned my crystal ball to pay for last week's heating-oil delivery.

Stanley A. Sussman,
Associate Professor,
Department of History,
Southern Connecticut
State College [12]

Tenure as the bulwark of academic freedom, impoverished professors only trying to help their fellow man, and irony with the unmistakable "there's nothing new under the sun" ring to it— an entirely predictable response. In fact, Drucker's suggestions seem eminently reasonable to me as far as they go. I'd only want to add the requirement that when a professor's contract is renewed he must reaffirm his allegiance to the values that are now supposedly protected by tenure.

Fritz Machlup has outlined these values as well as anyone could: teachers and scholars should be uninhibited in criticizing accepted theories, existing social, political, and economic institutions (including their own colleges and universities), and should be ready and willing to support colleagues whose critical acumen makes them unpopular. My only quibble is with the word "uninhibited" in that it can be read as a synonym for exhibitionistic. What is needed in

[12] *The Chronicle of Higher Education*, February 22, 1977.

academic life is more analysis, not more acting out.

As things now stand, professors feel justified spending their time writing memoranda on their natural authority and the ideal balance between core courses and elective esoterica. Abolishing tenure will not in itself transform them into Galileos, any more than preserving tenure has made them significantly more willing to challenge conventional wisdom. But because the peculiarities of the current contract system have come to seem both sign and shield of the professors' sense of specialness, it is hard for me to believe that they will be able to gain any new perspective on their individual careers, much less on the higher learning itself, as long as they are protected by tenure.

6

Conclusions

If we had got into the way of looking chiefly at those things, which Christ and his apostles and prophets chiefly insisted on, and so in judging of ourselves and others, chiefly regarding practical exercises and effects of grace . . . it would become fashionable for men to shew their Christianity, more by an amiable distinguished behavior, than by an abundant and excessive declaring their experiences; and we should get into the way of appearing lively in religion, more by being lively in the service of God and our generation, than by the liveliness and forwardness of our tongues, and making a business of proclaiming on house tops, with our mouths, the holy and eminent acts and

exercises of our own hearts; ... and religion
would be declared and manifested in such a way,
that instead of hardening spectators, and exceedingly promoting infidelity and atheism, would
above all things tend to convince men that there
is a reality in religion, and greatly awaken them,
and win them, by convincing their consciences of
the importance and excellency of religion. Thus
the light of professors would so shine before men,
that others seeing their good works, would glorify
their Father which is in heaven.[1]

WHEN JONATHAN EDWARDS argued that the reality and importance of religion needed to be dem-
onstrated, rather than merely advertised, he was
speaking to "professors" in the Calvinist sense—
the converted, the born-again. But if the word
"education" is substituted for "religion," his appeal to Christians can be read as an eloquent
summary of what "professors" in the academic
sense most need to hear. If faculty meetings were
marked by "amiable distinguished behavior" and
professors' testimony, whether in the classroom
or around the conference table, bore the stamp of
disinterested intelligence, it would do more for
the credibility of the higher learning than all the
pseudo-events designed to prove that only the

[1] John E. Smith, ed., *Jonathan Edwards: Religious Affections* (1746;
reprint ed., New Haven: Yale University Press, 1959), p. 461.

four-year liberal arts degree stands between American society and perdition.

My own faith in the notion that college degrees guarantee upward mobility, whether that mobility is a summer home on Martha's Vineyard or a firm grasp of higher values, has been severely shaken. And although I accept the general proposition that university-based research benefits mankind, I cannot see how, in itself, this research function justifies supporting higher education on anything like the current scale.

In fact the only plausible way I can see to argue for mass higher education is to begin with the proposition that it is a great advantage to be able to consider alternatives instead of seizing the first thought or opportunity that comes along, and to end with the assertion that colleges and universities are an excellent place to learn how to discriminate between competing goods. Justifying higher learning in terms of "life adjustment" is as unappealing as judging a curriculum by whether or not it builds character. Course descriptions such as the following leave one wondering why anyone would pay tuition to take off his clothes:

> EDSS 218XX *Shedding Old Skins: Human Life Styling for the Educator and Helping Professional*

> This is an opportunity for professionals to work on themselves. Our professional work is always a re-

flection of our personal lifestyles. The work we do is a function of what we are. The workshop will provide an intensive opportunity in a supportive setting for professional helpers to *help themselves* by shedding old skins (experiencing shifts in the usual ways we perceive, live, and work in the world). Participants will be helped to create more effective professional teaching and helping styles by creating richer, more holistic, integrated living styles. Workshop activities will include guided fantasies; stress reduction activities—relaxation, meditation, visualization, and autogenic training; personal empowerment experiences; aerobic exercise; nutritional assistance; role playing; Eastern perspectives on helping and teaching; energy awareness; empathy training; reaching deeper levels of consciousness; and dream interpretation. Activities will be grounded in rigorous conceptual study of Reich, Jung, May, Rogers, Singer, McCamy, Pelletier, and Leonard. Many activities and concepts can also be used in professional settings with clients and students. Permission by instructors. Enrollment Limit: 24 students.

When I suggest it is better to be able to reflect on alternatives, I am not talking about life-styles, but the ability to handle abstractions, really handle them—turn them over, even turn them inside out. I remain convinced that the way people interpret reality makes all the difference. As important as plagues and wars and elections may be in shaping history, what people think—about the nature of true virtue or the validity of IQ tests—is crucially important.

Taking college courses is obviously not the only way to sort out one's thoughts; some courses may have a muddling effect. Yet insofar as it is possible to imagine that the college curriculum helps students to see the difference between what it means to know something, and just making a stab at it, I think it is reasonable to believe that every American should have access to higher education in one form or another.

Studying Shakespeare (or Jonathan Edwards) is unlikely to increase a student's sense of being in control of his or her own life in quite the way that a course in practical accounting can. But in the long run Shakespeare and Edwards should do more to give the student a perspective on the human condition than learning how to enter debits and credits. Assuming that this perspective is what we look for in someone who is "well-educated," it would seem logical to ask whether a proposed reform will increase intellectual autonomy. If the answer is "no" or "only accidentally," the reform is trivial, or worse, a serious diversion of energy.

It is necessary to go beyond tinkering with the curriculum and revamping the catalog. We have to consider the need for genuine reformation. Not a Billy Graham television spectacular with a lot of choreographed holy rolling about values, but a new willingness by professors and their administrative apologists to get their mouths around some genuinely important yeas and nays.

Higher education is dominated by the spirit of the sure thing. Everyone gets guarantees: students are assured that their degrees are valuable, whether they are to be redeemed in cash or the coin of virtue; professors are told that they can count on a safe berth until sixty-five. Mounting evidence that degrees cost many people more than they are worth, that "tenure" may be another word for "immurement," has been met by "proclaiming on house tops." The only attempts to deal directly with a changing reality are the new litigiousness of students determined to get their money's worth and of professors concerned about job security.

It is pointless to yearn for the days when students and faculty knew their places and didn't behave like guardhouse lawyers or longshoremen. After all, as long as colleges and universities offer guarantees, no reasonable person would accept anything less than the advertised item. What *is* to the point now is to do everything possible to show that the ethos of the sure thing is antithetical to the spirit of critical intelligence. If faculty members are as convinced as they say they are that the application of critical intelligence is a great good in itself, and if they grow increasingly willing to acknowledge that this application is a risky business, they will have to turn from defending their status to more important issues.

It is possible to argue that because the intellectual lives of dedicated scholars are hard, their beds should be soft. But that seems as dubious a proposition as suggesting that only those who sleep on nails can know truth. The relationship between life-style and the life of the mind is ambiguous. Still there is every reason to fear that academics whose primary concern seems to be with their place in the universe, whether the weight given their specialty in the curriculum or the availability of subsidized faculty housing, are either already unfitted or gradually unfitting themselves for genuine intellectual adventure.

It is the ethos of the sure thing, then, that must be combated if higher education is to become more than an elaborate way of keeping young adults out of the job market and off the welfare rolls. And there is no way, as far as I can see, to manage this reformation from the top down. The well-managed college or university is a kind of never-never land where faculty members (and students) can indulge in their dreams of outlawry while enjoying the comforts of bourgeois family life.

For all his emphasis on demonstrating one's faith, Jonathan Edwards never believed that works alone would enable a person to enter the kingdom of heaven. Truly good works were the irresistible expression of a change of heart. A friend, even a minister, might not be able to distinguish between good behavior and a genuinely Christian demeanor. The best of human judges was bound to confuse appearances and spiritual realities.

Many secular analysts would argue that it makes relatively little difference in what "spirit" reforms are made, so long as the desired action follows. In specific cases, such instrumentalism seems appropriate—affirmative action for example. "Compliance" is defined as a matter of behavior; the emphasis of the programs is on works alone, not changing hearts. Yet their success depends ultimately on the power of experience to bring people to see the light. The assumption is that teaching (and teaching with) individuals of different races, sexes, or ethnic origins will, in the long run, make people less likely to prejudge.

Different kinds of reforms, however, require different strategies. Take the case of tenure. The experience of being deprived of tenure by administrative fiat is unlikely to make professors feel that they are increasingly responsible for shaping their own destiny. Before any change of faculty contract policy can be successful, the professors must see that the argument that tenure is crucial to the integrity of the academic enterprise may inadvertently do more to call that integrity into question than all the witch-hunters and red-baiters of the last fifty years.

In 1963 Suzanne Keller published an analysis of what happens when powerful special interest groups, "elites" as she calls them, "fail to keep pace with a world in continual flux—because of traditionalism, social distance, and social self-deception." Almost two decades later her words have particular relevance for anyone who would understand the plight of American academics.

> Their [an elite's] first important errors in judgment result in a gradually intensified suspicion of their powers and decline of public confidence. Sensing that they are losing hold on the public, the response of elites may be a redoubling of effort, or panic, or the first seeds of self-doubt and moral uncertainty. Moral uncertainty spreads as rapidly throughout human communities as does information about a new source of honey among communities of bees—in both instances, no words need be exchanged. Thereafter the stage is set for future errors, uneasily anticipated by the public."[2]

The academic community's declining public esteem is reflected in their growing malaise, what is most often referred to as "the faculty morale problem." It is this malaise that many believe can

[2] Suzanne Keller, *Beyond the Ruling Class: Strategic Elites in Modern Society* (New York: Random House, 1963), p. 245.

be alleviated by core curricula that implicitly reassert the central importance of the professoriate. Anyone who can teach core courses obviously has struck to the heart of the matter. Yet any strategy based on the notion that faculty members will look better in their own eyes once public esteem is restored is almost certainly doomed from the start, for public opinion only reflects the professors' misgivings about themselves.

Given Keller's predictions, one would expect that the current campaign to prove that academics have a unique understanding of true values would be met with increasing public uneasiness and anticipation of future errors. That's exactly what is happening. All the articles written recently about colleges and universities selling places to wealthy students are a case in point. They not only reflect the post-Watergate enthusiasm for exposing "the system," but represent a reaction to the shrill claims of the higher education establishment itself. It is almost as titillating to find the self-appointed guardians of adolescent character guilty of accepting bribes as it is to discover the minister in bed with a parishioner.

As far as I can see, the only effective way for professors to combat their self-doubts is to reaffirm their first principles and then accept the risks involved in trying to follow them. Afflicted by a professionally sanctioned decidophobia, faculty

members up until now have made crucial decisions by default, decisions they quite under-
standably prefer to ascribe to administrative in-
competence or public indifference. But if some
of them, perhaps the saving tenth, went beyond
the "yeah, yeah" reflex to test what it would
mean to weigh academic priorities according to
the same criteria they use to judge each other's
research, it would be the beginning of the end for
the sure-thing mentality that has dominated
American higher education for the last seventy-
five years.

In 1903 William James, who frequently quoted
Edwards's ideas about demonstrating faith in
support of his own pragmatism, published an article on "The Ph.D. Octopus." Deploring the enthusiasm for honorific titles "with which all Ger-
many is crawling" and which, as far as he could
tell, was primarily useful in enabling "one's wife
as well as one's self . . . to dazzle the servants,"
James was horrified to find that the taste for mer-
etricious honors had proved contagious and that
there was reason to fear that individuality was
"going to count for nothing" even among Americans "unless stamped and licensed and authenti-
cated by some title-giving machine." Universities, he felt, could play a crucial role in the fight
against "officialism and snobbery" by keeping
"truth and disinterested labor always in the fore-
ground" and treating "degrees as secondary inci-

dents," making it clear that "what they live for is to help men's souls, and not to decorate their persons with diplomas."[3]

Today, thanks largely to the academic community, James's worst fears about a spreading enthusiasm for degrees and titles have come true. It is hard to imagine accomplishing any significant academic reform without first attacking credential worship, starting with the bachelor's degree.

Specialized programs, whether in law or dental hygiene, do not undermine autonomy. Their existence may tempt students away from the study of logic or literature, the programs may be ill-conceived, they may be inadequate preparation for jobs, or wasteful in countless ways. But as long as they are entered into freely by individuals who have not been misled by false advertising, I see little reason to worry. The worth of whatever certificates or diplomas that are given out to graduates of these programs need not be taken on faith; it can be determined in the job market.

The debate between "vocationalism" and the liberal arts has mistakenly been regarded as a major struggle between diametrically opposed world views simply because study of the liberal arts has traditionally been identified with the four-year undergraduate degree. What this has meant is that anyone who argues for specialized

[3] William James, "The Ph.D. Octopus," *Harvard Monthly*, March 1903, pp. 8–9, 7.

programs has been cast as the enemy of liberal education, luring students away from English or history courses, into nursing or accounting. Once the sanctity of the bachelor's degree is questioned, vocationalism (or preprofessionalism) is not the enemy, it is simply an alternative.

Whether or not the bachelor's degree is awarded, some of those who enroll in college would be engaged in preparing themselves for specialized study. Professional or vocational schools would continue to shape their own entrance requirements. What would differ from the present confusion is that the students, whether *en route* to a profession or following their curiosity, would have their own ideas about what return they expected on their investment.

The bachelor's degree has served a normative function, establishing a correct age (eighteen to twenty-two) and a correct or at least preferred way (full-time residence) to be educated. At many schools, adult education is seen either as a means of increasing body count or as a pacification project (community relations), when in fact it probably makes more sense to think of it as the basic form—the normal pattern of higher education for people of all ages—with more specialized degree programs off on one side.

Currently those colleges and universities that have developed large continuing-education operations have done so primarily to take advantage of a new student market. The more prestigious, better-endowed schools, those least dependent on tuition dollars for their survival, have left the field to others. As the history professor who directs Princeton's "very modest" program for one hundred adults summarized the situation in *The Wall Street Journal:* "The falling birthrate isn't a matter of concern to this university. We're not hurting for students."

Given the tendency of academics to define "good form" in terms of current practices at Princeton or Smith, the only real hope for eliminating the bachelor's degree on principle (rather than by accident), and thereby creating a more rigorous and yet modest model of general education, is to begin at the most prestigious schools. Community colleges have, in effect, done away with the bachelor's degree, but their shrewd assessment of how to position themselves in the higher education market hasn't done anything to challenge credentialism. If anything, it has reinforced it by inventing a new credential, the associate's degree, and by giving people at four-year institutions still another reason for valuing the bachelor's degree that sets them apart.

There is a Catch-22. Those colleges and universities that could afford the courage of their convictions and, at least together, could figure out how to fill their classrooms without awarding bachelor's degrees, are the ones that feel the least pressure to change. On the scale of things, their degrees are worth something; they are not trying to establish a marketing position or prove anything in particular. The only crack in all this complacency is the moral uncertainty, demoralization, whatever you want to call it, of the professors themselves. Which brings me back to the thought that it is only the professors, potentially uneasy about sure things and willing to reconsider inherited and inherently self-interested wisdom, who can restore the integrity of the higher learning.

Former Secretary of Labor Willard Wirtz, writing in *The Boundless Resource: A Prospectus for an Education-Work Policy*, has suggested that "To love life greatly is to realize no less clearly that for many people it would make as much sense if life were lived the other way around: so that we came shuffling into it at age seventy-five or eighty; went first through those ten or fifteen years nobody has yet figured out the use for; moved after that rough initiation on to forty years of reasonably satisfying, if not easy, productiveness; entered then the doors to twelve or eighteen years of exciting learning and discovery; topped this off with a few years of love but little consequence; and had the doctor at the end of it pick us up by the heels and pat us goodbye instead of hello."[4]

---

[4] Willard Wirtz, *The Boundless Resource: A Prospectus for an Education-Work Policy* (Washington, D.C.: The New Republic Book Company, 1975), p. 7.

Short of such a radical turnaround, Wirtz and the twenty-four members of the National Manpower Institute have suggested that making provision for interspersing learning and earning is "the essential condition for an effective career as a worker, citizen, or human being,"[5] and they propose that every adult be entitled to five years of educational renewal opportunity.

Their proposal seems a more plausible way of encouraging support for the life of the mind while accomplishing broadly humane objectives than Kurt Vonnegut's suggestion that welfare recipients should be required to submit weekly book reports. Anyone who shudders to think of higher education's becoming the moral equivalent of the Civilian Conservation Corps should consider the extent to which our overgrown state college and university systems function to keep a significant percentage of the population out of the work force and off the streets. Why it is believed to be a higher calling to teach eighteen-year-olds with nothing better to do than un- or underemployed adults is hard to imagine, unless you prefer the illusion of promise to the realities of economic life.

Or unless you are wedded to the idea of the ultimate certifying power of the university. The fraud of credentialism is perhaps best exposed in the current enthusiasm for "life experience" credits, a means by which professors put the stamp of approval on an individual's extra-academic experiences. It is as if life only became real when translated into the language of course descriptions and credit hours.

Professors themselves have been carefully educated to accept credentialism as the way of the world. The Ph.D. supposedly is both a vocational degree *and* a reward for being able to contribute in an original way to the sum of human knowledge. The fact that few of those with doctorates have been trained to teach or have produced a thesis that is anything more than esoteric makework is generally felt to be beside the point. Academics' attitudes toward the Ph.D., like their attitudes toward tenure, reflect a deep confusion of professional and aristocratic values that only strengthens their faith in the power of titles and degrees.

David Riesman and Christopher Jencks have suggested, somewhat wistfully, that "the academic profession is now mature enough and powerful enough . . . that it no longer needs a protective tariff to maintain its share of the undergraduate market." They have proposed creating institutions in which academicians remain "the majority shareholders," but in which other groups have a substantial minority voice. "The aim would not be to *replace* the academic disciplines but to supplement them. The faculty would include substantial numbers of tenured members who were not scholars but doctors, lawyers, administrators, and so forth. The program would include not only regular academic courses in literature, psychology, and chemistry, but clinical experience and field work of various kinds."[6]

Riesman and Jencks fear seeming "visionary," but they seem to me not to have gone far enough. It is hard, I think, to be sanguine about hermaphrodite institutions dominated by "real" professors with an admixture of "others," presumably visiting artists and men and women "of affairs." Surely it would be better to make a concerted effort to build a faculty of intellectuals in the broadest sense of the word by breaking with aristocratic models of academic life as well as with some of the more narrowly professional ones, deemphasizing the Ph.D. as a prerequisite for appointment, rethinking patterns of faculty hiring, and doing away with tenure altogether.

In the course of trying to outline future directions for Bennington, the joint committee of trustees, faculty members, and alumni began by trying to characterize those teachers who had brought unusual vitality to the college. In its early years Bennington had been able to attract artists and intellectuals whom "reputable" insti-

[6] Christopher Jencks and David Riesman, *The Academic Revolution* (Garden City, N.Y.: Doubleday, 1968), p. 508.

tutions would not touch. Subsequently, as the visiting painter or the émigré philosopher became a familiar figure on more traditional campuses, Bennington went through its own process of self-correction, capitalizing on the boom years of the sixties to build a science building and hire Ivy League Ph.D.s.

This self-corrective impulse, supported by a rapid increase in the size of the student body, had the effect of flooding the faculty with professional academics, many of whom preferred the safe superiority of the nonpublisher, but who nonetheless presumed to judge and find wanting those anti-academic individuals and practices that had made Bennington a lively educational option during its first twenty-five years.

But it is not necessary to delve into the history of any one institution to see that a college or university in which tenured academics are the majority stockholders is apt to be a hostile environment for artists and intellectuals—at least if the latter are so bold as to imagine that their ideas about teaching and learning should be reflected in the way the school allocates its resources. Several years ago a feud between Edmund Wilson and the Modern Language Association brought out the professors' territorial feelings in a particularly striking way. Wilson had complained that the MLA's effort to produce authoritative texts through their Center for Editions of American

Authors was a boondoggle turning out pedantic, essentially unreadable books. In response the academicians published a booklet in which they asserted that "It must be obvious" that Wilson's "attack in *The New York Review of Books* . . . derives in part from the alarm of amateurs at seeing rigorous professional standards applied to a subject in which they have a vested interest. Here, at least, the issue is not in doubt. As the American learned world has come to full maturity since the second World War, a similar animus has shown itself and been discredited in field after field from botany to folklore. In the long run professional standards always prevail."[7]

Before academics can overcome their sense that they have a vested interest in all matters intellectual, they need to stop thinking of their own careers in these terms. As things now stand, most faculty members think about their futures in institution-bound ways, and as a result they are tempted to project upon a particular college or university a broad variety of destructive emotions. They are at once dependent and spiteful, grateful and furious. Their ability to look at the foibles of either their college or their colleagues with anything like dispassionate intelligence is minimal. And salary pressures, hiring freezes, all the manifestations of an academic bear market

[7] Quoted by Richard Ohmann, *English in America: A Radical View of the Profession* (New York: Oxford University Press, 1976), p. 38.

cannot help but exacerbate these unproductive feelings.

The officers of the American Association of University Professors have assumed that no one will speak up unless his or her job is secure. My own hunch would be that no one who puts much stock in job security is likely to speak up under any circumstances. In fact, given the likelihood that independent-minded professors will make their colleagues more uncomfortable than they do their deans or presidents, the thought of guaranteed employment at a particular college or university (and guaranteed unemployability elsewhere because senior ranks are tenured in) is apt to be inhibiting rather than inspiriting.

I believe that college and university teaching positions should be seen as honors to be enjoyed intermittently as a reward for proven accomplishments, and not as a means of supporting inoffensively bookish habits. The only real argument against interspersing teaching (or learning) with work outside academe is that distinguished scholars and researchers need continuous access to great libraries, specially equipped laboratories, and uninterrupted periods of time. Unquestionably this is true. But when only a very small proportion of American faculty members are actively engaged in scholarship or research, it seems bizarre, to say nothing of wasteful, to insist that all of their careers be modeled along scholarly lines.

By their own account only one-third of all professors publish anything at all. How many then would find their studies seriously hampered by regular involvement in jobs outside the university? Suppose that there are twenty-five thousand or even fifty thousand individuals in this "seriously hampered" category, isn't it possible to ensure that they can find appropriate working environments without being continuously employed as professors? In short, there has to be some way of supporting research without involving hundreds of thousands of people in career patterns that neither make sense for them or for their students.

The typical academic environment, in which students are taught by people who have made their own career choices once and for all, is probably not the best one for young adults pondering their own options. Even if they have no intention of staying in academe, students are likely to get the impression that careers are something you go to school to "get" and then you "have" for the next forty or fifty years. But if today's professors are inadequate or inappropriate models for adolescents, they will presumably have even less to offer mature adults returning to the classroom. It is not that I would expect academics to be career counselors. Yet unless you can feel that the way people think through a series of abstractions is wholly separate from the way they think about their personal options, it is troubling, to say the least, to contemplate a future in which forty-year-old students interested in reexamining their choices and assumptions are taught by professors who believe themselves set for life.

The post World War II baby boom has not only ensured that the number of forty-year-olds will soon be greater than the number of eighteen-year-olds, making adults an increasingly attractive target for those who market higher education, it virtually guarantees a "promotion squeeze" in the labor market itself. The effects of this squeeze will depend upon the general economic climate: in a static or recessionary period, job dissatisfaction will grow; under more favorable circumstances midlife career switching will become more popular. In either case the proportion of people between thirty-five and forty-five who are interested in returning to school, whether to find a sense of fulfillment they can't get from their jobs or to train themselves for new careers, will almost certainly increase. And the thought of these people being taught by peers who have dedicated their lives to the sure thing is disquieting.

Even if you set aside the question of what students need and concentrate on their teachers' best interests, much the same conclusions suggest themselves. A full professor who is paid $35,000 a year for carrying on his or her specialized study and teaching might be quite willing to settle for protracted studentless stretches at a lower salary. Others, creative artists, for example, who find a certain amount of regular contact with students stimulating, might contract to work only one-third or one-quarter time on a regular basis. These arrangements are common enough, but they are generally regarded as the exception when perhaps they should be the rule.

Even at Bennington, where the number of artists (and the distance from New York) has from the beginning made the logic of part-time and short-term appointments clear, there are repeated battles over the "commuter question." Those faculty members who teach full time and live nearby feel that they are bearing more than their fair share of the institutional burden. They are the ones who must sit on faculty curriculum committees and haggle over who should get tenure and who should not get degrees, while their colleagues, the commuters, have a maddening tendency to teach their students and get the hell out.

After the annual battle a few years ago, one of the commuters, a man of barely thirty, was taken to Putnam Memorial Hospital in Bennington by friends who feared he was suffering a heart attack. Fortunately an emergency room physician had the presence of mind to ask if anything had upset him recently. It turned out that he was having an adrenaline attack—his body's defenses had mobilized so effectively against collegial pressure that he suffered from acute chest pain, irregular pulse, difficulty in breathing, in short, the symptoms of something more alarming than professorial rage.

It is possible that an entire faculty made up of commuters, people who expect to move back and forth between academic life and some other work, might be dominated by a spirit of "teach your courses and get the hell out." Their energy for reforming a particular college or university would necessarily be limited. But I think this lack of energy would be more than compensated for by a regularly renewed sense of proportion.

It is surely wrong to imagine that interested outsiders, what sociologists call "participant observers," know less about what is going on than insiders do. On the contrary, a certain edge of outsideness probably sharpens everyone's wits. Moreover, insiders often have a good reason for preferring not to understand a particular situation. Cycled faculty members might be able to afford to be more perceptive than those who have dug in for the duration.

Still there is clearly a difference between understanding a situation and taking responsibility for coping with it. Wouldn't the new-style commuters have less incentive to work through difficulties and see projects to completion? Here I think the answer must be yes and no. The reform-ist spirit that may grow out of a sense of entrapment—we're all in this together and better do something, anything, to keep our spirits up—would be lost. What would be gained is a faculty with experience in the extra-academic world to draw upon, people impatient with the ever tasteful "that's the way we do things around here."

An additional advantage of thinking in terms of career cycles (instead of trajectories) is that it would make it possible for many more faculty members to serve as deans and admissions officers without forever losing their credibility with colleagues. Today professors who accept deanships become suspect, and any new points of view they might bring back to faculty debates tend to be discounted accordingly. As one professor commented on her refusal to accept an administrative appointment: "Query: What does the half-time rotating assistant dean do when not rotating? Answer: He twists gently in the wind." A deliberate confusion of roles seems one of the best ways of enlarging the sympathies of current academics, enabling them to see that when they proclaim their own superiority from the housetops they "exceedingly promote" little except antagonism.

If the bachelor's degree and tenure were eliminated or significantly modified in the conviction that sure things have no place in higher education, other changes would become inescapable.

Convictions tend to spill over in unexpected ways, although at least a few spillovers are easy enough to predict.

Faculty members without vested interests in a particular department or institution would be less inclined than they are now to see curriculum debate as an opportunity to redefine orthodoxy and reassert their priestly status. Confronted by a far from captive audience, they would have to concentrate instead on exploring alternatives, setting forth competing ideas in order to educate their students, and themselves. It may sound elitist to say that those who cannot follow the outlines of such a debate do not belong in institutions of higher education. But it is really less discriminatory in the long run than implying that everyone can be bettered by a mysterious process that involves the laying on of culture and tax dollars.

In a similar fashion the public relations activities of colleges and universities would be redesigned to provide information instead of selling the green grass and the great men. Looking through a Radcliffe newsletter a few years ago, Diana Trilling commented that the "self-approval it managed to communicate without outright boastfulness was not unfamiliar to me from other promotional material sent to me by various colleges through the years, and not for the first time it made me wonder whether all educational institutions had to admire themselves this inordinately."[8] The answer, it would seem, must be no.

Other changes, decisions about what to do with dormitories and student unions once there is no longer a captive undergraduate population, may prove even more difficult to accomplish than the more ideological reforms. Yet if any segment of American society has the resources, in every sense of the word, to make choices about its future, it should be the academic community.

Unfortunately, up until now, its members have chosen to ignore impertinent questions, secure in the knowledge that what is worth saying has already been said. I certainly don't claim originality in suggesting that the bachelor's degree be abolished or that faculty members be recruited who regard teaching on the college level as a signal honor and an intermittent occupation. At best these suggestions represent first steps in eliminating the spirit of the sure-thing.

I can imagine what I'd hope Harvard to be like, or Bennington, or the University of Vermont; certainly I would want them to be quite different from the way they are now *and* from each other. But it seems preposterous to spend five chapters arguing that teaching faculty should be held responsible for shaping their particular institutions,

[8] Diana Trilling, "Daughters of the Middle Class," *Harper's*, April 1977, p. 92.

and then to turn around in Chapter 6 and offer my own thoughts as the last word. I would be more than satisfied to feel that I had helped to subvert professorial complacency—that worship of good form that tempts one to see resemblances between American academics today and the British in the Bengal Club at the end of the *raj*.

Professors not only have their own ideas about what is *pukka*, they have their own imperial dreams and their own native populations—the students. But what makes them most reminiscent of the curry colonels bemoaning the course of empire is their eagerness to cover their mixed motives and vested interests with a lot of high-minded talk about the preservation of ineffable values.

Perron, the hero of Paul Scott's estimable *Raj Quartet,* is a British academic who finds himself in India during the closing days of World War II. He argues that there is a crucial difference between being serious about a serious situation and being serious about oneself in that situation. Perron has come to feel that those remnants of the *raj* left in 1945 need to be laughed at, as much for their own good as anything else. Laughter, as he sees it, is a way of expressing concern—as well as perspective.

In a climactic scene, Perron suggests that the "empire and all that God-the-Father-the-*raj* was a lot of insular middle- and lower-class shit . . .

Kiplingesque double-talk that transformed India from a place where plain ordinary greedy Englishmen carved something out for themselves to balance out the more tedious consequences of the law of primogeniture, into one where they appeared go to voluntarily into exile for the good of their souls and the uplift of the native."[9]

The double-talk of degrees and tenure is hardly less self-serving. Academics protect their own status under the guise of teaching true values, and seem convinced that a self-imposed exile from what they regard as the "real world" entitles them to special privileges and exemptions. Paul Scott allowed his academic hero to have the best lines *and* the last laugh. It remains to be seen whether American professors will do nearly so well for themselves.

[9] Paul Scott, *A Division of the Spoils* (New York: William Morrow, 1976), pp. 208–9.

Index